A HISTORICAL READER

The
American
WEST

D0171173

nextext

Table of Contents

PART I: EXPLORING THE WILDERNESS

1894
from *The Mountains of California* 12
By John Muir
The founder of the Sierra Club celebrates the beauty of Yosemite Valley.

Prehistory
The Migrations of the Hopi 16
By Frank Waters
Hopi elders relate ancient traditions about the legendary wanderings of their clans from the ancestral homeland in the Southwest.

1539–1542
from *The Journey of Coronado* 20
By Pedro de Castañeda
Searching for the Seven Cities of Cibola, legendary Indian cities of fabulous wealth, Coronado's men are amazed by the vastness of the Great Plains.

1804–1806
The Expedition of Lewis and Clark 25
By Thomas Jefferson and Meriwether Lewis
Jefferson's letter of instruction to Lewis, an entry from the expedition's journal, and Lewis's first report on his return present the goals and accomplishments of this expedition in opening the West to American settlement.

1810
Colter's Run **35**
By John Bradbury

John Colter, one of the earliest of the mountain men, is forced to literally run for his life after being captured by Indians.

1820s
Living with the Indians **40**
By James P. Beckwourth

In his autobiography, an African-American mountain man describes how he was adopted by Crow Indians.

1873
Mountain Jim **47**
By Isabella Bird

An Englishwoman traveling in the Rockies meets one of the last of the mountain men.

Photo Album: Encountering the Wilderness **51**

PART II: ESTABLISHING COMMUNITIES

1770s–1840s
Spanish California **58**
By Guadalupe Vallejo

A member of an old Spanish family presents an affectionate picture of life on the missions and ranches during the period when the Spanish and Mexicans governed California.

1839–1846
Early Texas **66**
By Frances Cook Lipscomb Van Zandt

*An American who settled in the Lone Star Republic
during its brief existence describes her life there.*

1846
The Donner Party **72**
By Patrick Breen

*The tragic story of a group of emigrants trapped by
winter in the Sierra Nevadas is glimpsed in a diary kept
by one of the survivors.*

1847
The Morman Migration **76**
By Brigham Young

*In his journal, the leader of the Mormon pioneers
describes their journey to the Valley of the Great
Salt Lake.*

1849
**A Woman's Trip Across
the Plains in 1849** **83**
By Catherine Haun

*A woman who traveled from Iowa to the California gold
fields recalls her journey.*

1881
Gunfight at the O.K. Corral **97**
From *The Tombstone Epitaph* and inquest testimony

*A local newspaper and eyewitnesses present differing
accounts of the most famous shootout in frontier history.*

1905
African Americans in Oklahoma Territory 102
By Booker T. Washington

*A famous educator visits one of the all-black communities
established in the West in the 1880s.*

Photo Album: Homes and Families............................107

PART III: MAKING A LIVING

1851–1852
Mining in California..116
By Louisa Clappe

*In a letter to her sister back home, a woman
provides an account of the early days of the California
Gold Rush.*

1867–1880s
Cattle Drives..122
By Joseph G. McCoy

*The work of the cowboy is described by one of the
pioneers of the cattle business.*

Late 1860s–1882
Chinese Workers 127
From Grenville Dodge's How We Built the Union Pacific
Railroad, An English-Chinese Phrase Book, *and the* Chinese
Exclusion Act

*Three documents convey the problems encountered by
Chinese immigrants to the West in the late 1800s.*

Late 1870s
Destruction of the Buffalo **133**
By Frank H. Mayer

*A former buffalo hunter recalls how he and the others
in his trade "killed the golden goose."*

1870s
Farming on the Great Plains **138**
By Hamlin Garland

*A writer describes the joys and sorrows of his youth on
a frontier farm.*

Photo Album: Westerners at Work **146**

PART IV: PRESERVING A HERITAGE

1844
Letters and Notes on the
North American Indians **154**
By George Catlin

*A painter who sought to "rescue from oblivion" the
appearance and customs of the Native Americans
records his observations and experiences gathered
during travels in the West.*

1881
from *A Century of Dishonor* **160**
By Helen Hunt Jackson

*A writer presents her famous indictment of a long history
of mistreatment of the Indians by the government and
white settlers in the West.*

1907

The Conservation of Natural Resources 167

By Theodore Roosevelt

*In a message to Congress, President Roosevelt reports
on the success of his conservation programs.*

1933

The Indian View of Nature 172

By Luther Standing Bear

*A Lakota Sioux leader explores the differences between
Indian and white views of nature.*

Photo Album: A Vanishing World 180

PART V: INTERPRETING THE PAST

1893

The Significance of the Frontier
in American History 188

By Frederick Jackson Turner

*A historian presents his landmark thesis that the
experience of the frontier fundamentally shaped
American political institutions, society, and character.*

1931

from The Great Plains 194

By Walter Prescott Webb

*A historian details specific effects of the landscape and
climate of the Great Plains on people's respect for law,
people's political outlook, and the attitudes of women.*

1994
A Saga of Families 206
By Kathleen Neils Conzen

*A historian examines themes of "family, kinship, and
community" in* My Darling Clementine, Ford's *classic
film version of the gunfight at the O.K.Corral.*

Photo Album: The Wild West **215**

Chronology 220

Acknowledgements 222

Index 223

*Throughout the reader, vocabulary words appear in boldface
type and are footnoted. Specialized or technical words and phrases
appear in lightface type and are footnoted.*

Exploring the Wilderness

from

The Mountains of California

BY JOHN MUIR

The most immediately obvious feature of the American West is the grandeur of the landscape, here evoked by naturalist John Muir (1838–1914). Before settling down in California's Yosemite Valley in 1868, Muir spent years wandering thousands of miles on foot through the American wilderness observing wildlife. Muir dedicated his life to preserving the natural beauties of the West from commercial exploitation. In 1892 he organized the Sierra Club, which continues to work for the protection of wilderness areas. In his book The Mountains of California *(1894), Muir celebrated the beauty of Yosemite, which he had helped establish as a national park in 1890.*

Arriving by the Panama steamer, I stopped one day in San Francisco and then inquired for the nearest way out of town. "But where do you want to go?" asked the man to whom I had applied for this important information.

"To any place that is wild," I said. This reply startled him. He seemed to fear I might be crazy and therefore the sooner I was out of town the better, so he directed me to the Oakland ferry.

So on the first of April, 1868, I set out afoot for Yosemite. It was the bloom-time of the year over the lowlands and coast ranges; the landscapes of the Santa Clara Valley were fairly drenched with sunshine, all the air was quivering with the songs of the meadow-larks, and the hills were so covered with flowers that they seemed to be painted. Slow indeed was my progress through these glorious gardens, the first of the California **flora**[1] I had seen. Cattle and cultivation were making few scars as yet, and I wandered enchanted in long wavering curves, knowing by my pocket map that Yosemite Valley lay to the east and that I should surely find it.

Looking eastward from the summit of the Pacheco Pass one shining morning, a landscape was displayed that after all my wanderings still appears as the most beautiful I have ever beheld. At my feet lay the Great Central Valley of California, level and flowery, like a lake of pure sunshine, forty or fifty miles wide, five hundred miles long, one rich furred garden of yellow Compositae.[2] And from the eastern boundary of this vast golden flower-bed rose the mighty Sierra, miles in height, and so gloriously colored and so radiant, it seemed not clothed with light, but wholly composed of it, like the wall of some **celestial**[3] city.

Along the top and extending a good way down, was a rich pearl-gray belt of snow; below it a belt of blue and dark purple, marking the extension of the forests; and stretching along the base of the range a broad belt of

---

[1] **flora**—plants.

[2] Compositae—flowering plants of a large family that includes daisies, asters, marigolds, dandelions, and sunflowers.

[3] **celestial**—heavenly.

rose-purple; all these colors, from the blue sky to the yellow valley smoothly blending as they do in a rainbow, making a wall of light **ineffably**[4] fine.

Then it seemed to me that the Sierra should be called, not the Nevada or Snowy Range, but the Range of Light. And after ten years of wandering and wondering in the heart of it, rejoicing in its glorious floods of light, the white beams of the morning streaming through the passes, the noonday radiance on the crystal rocks, the flush of the alpenglow,[5] and the **irised**[6] spray of countless waterfalls, it still seems above all others the Range of Light.

In general views no mark of man is visible upon it, nor anything to suggest the wonderful depth and grandeur of its sculpture. . . . Nevertheless the whole range five hundred miles long is furrowed with cañons 2,000 to 5,000 feet deep, in which once flowed majestic glaciers, and in which now flow and sing the bright rejoicing rivers. . . .

The most famous and **accessible**[7] of these cañon valleys, and also the one that presents their most striking and sublime features on the grandest scale, is the Yosemite, situated in the basin of the Merced River at an elevation of 4,000 feet above the level of the sea. It is about seven miles long, half a mile to a mile wide, and nearly a mile deep in the solid granite flank of the range. The walls are made up of rocks, mountains in size, partly separated from each other by side cañons, and they are so **sheer**[8] in front, and so compactly and harmoniously arranged on a level floor, that the Valley, comprehensively seen, looks like an immense hall or temple lighted from above.

---

[4] **ineffably**—inexpressibly.

[5] alpenglow—reddish glow often seen on mountaintops shortly before sunrise or after sunset.

[6] **irised**—rainbow colored.

[7] **accessible**—easily reachable.

[8] **sheer**—nearly perpendicular; steep.

But no temple made with hands can compare with Yosemite. Every rock in its walls seems to glow with life. Some lean back in majestic repose; others, absolutely sheer or nearly so for thousands of feet, advance beyond their companions in thoughtful attitudes, giving welcome to storms and calms alike, seemingly aware, yet heedless, of everything going on about them. Awful in stern, immovable majesty, how softly these rocks are adorned, and how fine and reassuring the company they keep: their feet among beautiful groves and meadows, their brows in the sky, a thousand flowers leaning confidingly against their feet, bathed in floods of water, floods of light, while the snow and waterfalls, the winds and avalanches and clouds shine and sing and wreathe about them as the years go by, and myriads of small winged creatures—birds, bees, butterflies—give glad animation and help to make all the air into music.

Down through the middle of the Valley flows the crystal Merced, River of Mercy, peacefully quiet, reflecting lilies and trees and the onlooking rocks; things frail and fleeting and types of endurance meeting here and blending in countless forms, as if into this one mountain mansion Nature had gathered her choicest treasures, to draw her lovers into close and confiding communion with her.

QUESTIONS TO CONSIDER

1. Why did Muir think that the Sierra Nevada Mountains should be called "the Range of Light"?

2. Recalling his journey to Yosemite, Muir observed, "Cattle and cultivation were making few scars as yet." What outlook does this statement reveal?

3. What values did Muir see in the wilderness?

The Migrations of the Hopi

BY FRANK WATERS

The first explorers of the American West were the Indians. In their oral traditions, the Hopi people of the Southwest preserve an account of their early migrations. The Hopi believe that human beings have occupied a series of worlds, each less good than the preceding one. The present Fourth World "is not all beautiful and easy like the previous ones. It has height and depth, heat and cold, beauty and barrenness." After they emerged into the Fourth World, the Hopi clans began a series of migrations outward from their ancestral homeland. In The Book of the Hopi, *anthropologist Frank Waters recorded these traditions, which had been taken down from a group of Hopi elders and translated into English.*

And now before Másaw[1] turned his face from them and became invisible, he explained that every clan must make four directional migrations before they all arrived at their common, permanent home. They must go to the

---

[1] Másaw—divine being appointed by the Creator as the caretaker of the Fourth World.

ends of the land—west, south, east, and north—to the farthest *páso* (where the land meets the sea) in each direction. Only when the clans had completed these four movements, rounds, or steps of their migration could they come together again, forming the pattern of the Creator's universal plan.

That is the way it was. Some clans started to the south, others to the north, retraced their routes to turn east and west, and then back again. All their routes formed a great cross whose center, *Túwanasavi* (Center of the Universe), lay in what is now the Hopi country in the southwestern part of the United States, and whose arms reached to the four directional *pásos*. As they turned at each of these extremeties they formed of this great cross a **swastika**,[2] either clockwise or counter-clockwise, corresponding to the movement of the earth or of the sun. And then when their migrations slowed as they reached their permanent home, they formed spirals and circles, ever growing smaller. All these patterns formed by their four migrations are the basic **motifs**[3] of the symbols still found today in their pottery and basketware, on their *kachina*[4] rattles and altar boards.

Often one clan would come upon the ruins of a village built by a preceding clan and find on the mound broken pieces of pottery circling to the right or to the left, indicating which way the clan had gone. Throughout the continent these countless ruins and mounds covered with broken pottery are still being discovered. They constitute what people call now their **title**[5] to the land. Everywhere, too, the clans carved on rocks their signatures, pictographs and **petroglyphs**[6] which identified

---

[2] **swastika**—cross with arms bent at right angles.

[3] **motifs**—recurrent themes.

[4] The Hopi believe that the kachinas are the ancestors of human beings.

[5] **title**—claim of ownership.

[6] **petroglyphs**—carvings or line drawings on rocks made by ancient people.

them, revealed what round of their migration they were on, and related the history of the village.

Still the migrations continued. Some clans forgot in time the commands of Másaw, settling in tropical climates where life was easy, and developing beautiful cities of stone that were to decay and crumble into ruin. Other clans did not complete all four of their migrations before settling into their permanent home, and hence lost their religious power and standing. Still others persisted, keeping open the doors on top of their heads.[7] These were the ones who finally realized the purpose and the meaning of their four migrations.

For these migrations were themselves purification ceremonies, weeding out through generations all the **latent**[8] evil brought from the previous Third World. Man could not **succumb**[9] to the comfort and luxury given him by **indulgent**[10] surroundings, for then he lost the need to rely upon the Creator. Nor should he be frightened even by the **polar**[11] extremities of the earth, for there he learned that the power given him by the Creator would still sustain him. So, by traveling to the farthest extremities of the land during their four migrations, these chosen people finally came to settle on the vast **arid**[12] plateau that stretches between the Colorado and Rio Grande Rivers.

Many other people today wonder why these people chose an area **devoid**[13] of running water to irrigate their sparse crops. The Hopi people know that they were led here so that they would have to depend upon the scanty

---

[7] doors on top of their heads—The Hopi believe that the earliest human beings were able to communicate with the Creator through soft spots on the tops of their heads.

[8] **latent**—present but hidden.

[9] **succumb**—surrender.

[10] **indulgent**—comfortable.

[11] polar—arctic and antarctic.

[12] **arid**—dry.

[13] **devoid**—completely lacking.

rainfall which they must evoke with their power and prayer, and so preserve always that knowledge and faith in the supremacy of their Creator who had brought them to this Fourth World after they had failed in three previous worlds.

This, they say, is their supreme title to this land, which no secular[14] power can refute.

---

[14] secular—worldly.

QUESTIONS TO CONSIDER

1. What guided the Hopi in their explorations?

2. What did the migration records left by the Hopi mean to later travelers?

3. Why did the Hopi choose to live in a difficult environment?

from

The Journey of Coronado

BY PEDRO DE CASTAÑEDA

The Great Plains is the vast region of dry flatlands extending eastward from the Rocky Mountains. The first Europeans to see the Great Plains were the Spaniards who accompanied Francisco de Coronado (c. 1510–1554) on his expedition into the Southwest between 1539 and 1542. Coronado and his army were sent by the Spanish viceroy in Mexico to search for the Seven Cities of Cibola, legendary Indian cities of fabulous wealth. The cities were, in fact, the dwellings of the Pueblo Indian peoples. Although they did not locate any treasure, Coronado and his men saw the Grand Canyon and probably traveled as far as what is now Kansas before turning back. The expedition introduced horses into the American West and opened the region to Spanish colonization. The Journey of Coronado was written by Pedro de Castañeda (1510–1570), who accompanied the expedition.

Chapter VIII
Which describes some remarkable things that were seen on the plains, with a description of the bulls.

My silence was not without mystery and dissimulation[1] when earlier I spoke of the plains and of the things of which I will give a detailed account in this chapter, where all these things may be found together; for these things were remarkable and something not seen in other parts. I dare to write of them because I am writing at a time when many men are still living who saw them and who will **vouch**[2] for my account. Who could believe that 1,000 horses and 500 of our cows and more than 5,000 rams and ewes and more than 1,500 friendly Indians and servants, in traveling over those plains, would leave no more trace where they had passed than if nothing had been there—nothing—so that it was necessary to make piles of bones and cow dung now and then, so that the rear guard could follow the army. The grass never failed to become erect after it had been trodden down, and, although it was short, it was as fresh and straight as before.

Another thing was a heap of cow bones, a crossbow shot long,[3] or a very little less, almost twice a man's height in places, and some 18 feet or more wide, which was found on the edge of a salt lake in the southern part, and this in a region where there are no people who could have made it. The only explanation of this which could be suggested was that the waves which the north winds must make in the lake had piled up the bones of the cattle which had died in the lake, when the old and weak ones who went into the water were unable to get out. The

---

[1] dissimulation—disguise.

[2] **vouch**—provide proof.

[3] crossbow shot long—distance traveled by the bolt shot from a crossbow, a medieval weapon. The crossbow had a range of about 1,000 feet.

noticeable thing is the number of cattle that would be necessary to make such a pile of bones.

Now that I wish to describe the appearance of the bulls,[4] it is to be noticed first that there was not one of the horses that did not take flight when he saw them first, for they have a narrow, short face, the brow two palms across from eye to eye, the eyes sticking out at the side, so that, when they are running, they can see who is following them. They have very long beards, like goats, and when they are running they throw their heads back with the beard dragging on the ground. There is a sort of girdle[5] round the middle of the body. The hair is very woolly, like a sheep's, very fine, and in front of the girdle the hair is very long and rough like a lion's. They have a great hump, larger than a camel's. The horns are short and thick, so that they are not seen much above the hair. In May they change the hair in the middle of the body for a down,[6] which makes perfect lions of them. They rub against the small trees in the little ravines to shed their hair, and they continue this until only the down is left, as a snake changes his skin. They have a short tail, with a bunch of hair at the end. When they run, they carry it erect like a scorpion. It is worth noticing that the little calves are red and just like ours, but they change their color and appearance with time and age.

Another strange thing was that all the bulls that were killed had their left ears slit, although these were whole when young. The reason for this was a puzzle that could not be guessed. The wool ought to make good cloth on account of its fineness, although the color is not good, because it is the color of buriel.[7]

Another thing worth noticing is that the bulls traveled without cows in such large numbers that nobody

---

[4] bulls—buffalo.

[5] girdle—belt.

[6] down—soft fur.

[7] buriel—coarse gray woolen cloth.

could have counted them, and so far away from the cows that it was more than 40 leagues[8] from where we began to see the bulls to the place where we began to see the cows. The country they traveled over was so level and smooth that if one looked at them the sky could be seen between their legs, so that if some of them were at a distance they looked like smooth-trunked pines whose tops joined, and if there was only one bull it looked as if there were four pines. When one was near them, it was impossible to see the ground on the other side of them. The reason for all this was that the country seemed as round as if a man should imagine himself in a three-pint measure, and could see the sky at the edge of it, about a crossbow shot from him, and even if a man only lay down on his back he lost sight of the ground.

I have not written about other things which were seen nor made any mention of them, because they were not of so much importance, although it does not seem right for me to remain silent concerning the fact that they **venerate**[9] the sign of the cross in the region where the settlements have high houses. For at a spring which was in the plain near Acuco they had a cross two palms high and as thick as a finger, made of wood with a square twig for its crosspiece, and many little sticks decorated with feathers around it, and numerous withered flowers, which were the offerings. In a graveyard outside the village at Tutahaco there appeared to have been a recent burial. Near the head there was another cross made of two little sticks tied with cotton thread, and dry withered flowers. It certainly seems to me that in some way they must have received some light from the cross of Our Redeemer, Christ, and it may have come by way of India, from whence they proceeded.

---

[8] 40 leagues—120 miles (a league equals three miles).
[9] **venerate**—regard as holy.

QUESTIONS TO CONSIDER

1. Why did Castañeda "dare to write" of the extraordinary regions through which Coronado's army had passed?

2. Why was it necessary for Coronado's army to create markers to guide their rear guard?

3. How did Castañeda explain the crosslike ornaments created by the Indians?

4. What is Castañeda's overall impression of the landscape of the West?

The Expedition of Lewis and Clark

**BY THOMAS JEFFERSON AND
MERIWETHER LEWIS**

*In the spring of 1804, a group of approximately fifty men led by
Meriwether Lewis (1774–1809) and William Clark (1770–1838)
left St. Louis and journeyed up the Missouri River. They had been
commissioned by President Thomas Jefferson to search for the
Northwest Passage, a possible water route across the continent to
the Pacific Ocean. The expedition went up the Missouri to its headwaters, crossed the mountains, and reached the Pacific, returning to
St. Louis in the fall of 1806. The expedition of Lewis and Clark was
a critical step in opening the West to American settlement. The first
of the following documents dealing with the expedition is Jefferson's
letter of instruction to Lewis; the second is an entry by Lewis from
the expedition's journal; and the third is Lewis's letter to Jefferson
announcing the successful return of the expedition to St. Louis.
(The original spelling and punctuation of Lewis's journal entry and
letter have been retained.)*

Letter from President Thomas Jefferson

To Meriwether Lewis, esquire, captain of the first regiment of infantry of the United States of America:

The object of your mission is to explore the Missouri River, and such principal streams of it, as, by its course and communication with the waters of the Pacific Ocean, whether the Columbia, Oregon, Colorado, or any other river, may offer the most direct and **practicable**[1] water-communication across the continent, for the purposes of commerce.

Beginning at the mouth of the Missouri, you will take observations of latitude and longitude, at all remarkable points on the river, and especially at the mouths of rivers, at rapids, at islands, and other places and objects distinguished by such natural marks and characters, of a **durable**[2] kind, as that they may with certainty be recognised hereafter. The courses of the river between these points of observation may be supplied by the compass, the log-line, and by time, corrected by the observations themselves. The variations of the needle,[3] too, in different places, should be noticed.

The interesting points of the portage[4] between the heads[5] of the Missouri, and of the water offering the best communication with the Pacific ocean, should also be fixed by observation; and the course of that water to the ocean, in the same manner as that of the Missouri.

The commerce which may be carried on with the people inhabiting the line[6] you will pursue, renders a knowledge of those people important. You will therefore **endeavor**[7] to make yourself acquainted, as far as a

---

[1] **practicable**—workable.

[2] **durable**—lasting.

[3] needle—compass needle.

[4] portage—ground between navigable waterways over which boats must be carried.

[5] heads—headwaters; sources.

[6] line—line of march, that is, the expedition's route.

[7] **endeavor**—make it a goal.

diligent pursuit of your journey shall admit, with the names of the nations and their numbers;

The extent and limits of their possessions;

Their relations with other tribes or nations;

Their language, traditions, monuments;

Their ordinary occupations in agriculture, fishing, hunting, war, arts, and the implements for these;

Their food, clothing, and domestic accommodations:[8]

The diseases prevalent among them, and the remedies they use;

Moral and physical circumstances which distinguish them from the tribes we know;

Peculiarities in their laws, customs, and dispositions;[9]

And articles of commerce they may need or furnish, and to what extent.

And, considering the interest which every nation has in extending and strengthening the authority of reason and justice among the people around them, it will be useful to acquire what knowledge you can of the state of morality, religion, and information among them; as it may better enable those who may endeavor to civilize and instruct them, to adapt their measures to the existing notions and practices of those on whom they are to operate.

Other objects worthy of notice will be;

The soil and face of the country, its growth and vegetable productions, especially those not of the United States;

The animals of the country generally, and especially those not known in the United States;

The remains and accounts of any which may be deemed rare or extinct;

The mineral productions of every kind, but more particularly metals, limestone, pit-coal,[10] and saltpeter;[11]

---

[8] domestic accommodations—housing.

[9] dispositions—characteristic attitudes.

[10] pit-coal—coal deposits.

[11] saltpeter—deposits of potassium nitrate, used in making gunpowder.

salines and mineral waters,[12] noting temperature of the last, and such circumstances as may indicate their character;

Volcanic appearances;

Climate, as characterized by the thermometer, by the proportion of rainy, cloudy, and clear days; by lightning, hail, snow, ice; by the access [and] recess[13] of frost; by the winds prevailing at different seasons; the dates at which particular plants put forth, or lose their flower or leaf; times of appearance of particular birds, reptiles or insects.

In all your intercourse[14] with the natives, treat them in the most friendly and conciliatory manner which their own conduct will admit; allay all jealousies[15] as to the object of your journey; satisfy them of its innocence; make them acquainted with the position, extent, character, peaceable and commercial dispositions of the United States; of our wish to be neighborly; friendly, and useful to them, and of our dispositions to a commercial intercourse with them; confer with them on the points most convenient as mutual emporiums,[16] and the articles of most desirable interchange for them and us. If a few of their influential chiefs, within practicable distance, wish to visit us, arrange such a visit with them, and furnish them with authority to call on our officers on their entering the United States, to have them conveyed to this place at the public expense. If any of them should wish to have some of their young people brought up with us, and taught such arts as may be useful to them, we will receive, instruct, and take care of them. Such a mission, whether of influential chiefs, or of young people, would give some security to your own party. Carry with you

---

[12] salines and mineral waters—salt deposits and mineral springs.

[13] access [and] recess—onset and withdrawal.

[14] intercourse—communication.

[15] allay all jealousies—ease all fears.

[16] emporiums—marketplaces.

some matter of the kine-pox;[17] inform those of them with whom you may be of its **efficacy**[18] as a preservative from the smallpox, and instruct and encourage them in the use of it. This may be especially done wherever you winter. As it is impossible for us to foresee in what manner you will be received by those people, whether with hospitality or hostility, so is it impossible to prescribe the exact degree of **perseverance**[19] with which you are to pursue your journey. We value too much the lives of citizens to offer them to probable destruction. Your numbers will be sufficient to secure you against the unauthorized opposition of individuals, or of small parties; but if a superior force, authorized, or not authorized, by a nation, should be **arrayed**[20] against your further passage, and inflexibly determined to arrest it, you must decline its further pursuit and return. In the loss of yourselves we should lose also the information you will have acquired. By returning safely with that, you may enable us to renew the essay[21] with better calculated means. To your own **discretion**,[22] therefore, must be left the degree of danger you may risk, and the point at which you should decline, only saying, we wish you to err on the side of your safety, and to bring back your party safe, even if it be with less information.

Thomas Jefferson

President of the United States of America

from The Journals of Lewis and Clark
Wednesday, August 14th, 1805

In order to give Capt. Clark time to reach the forks of Jefferson's river I concluded to spend this day at the

---

[17] kine-pox—cowpox, a mild disease of cattle, caused by a virus once used to vaccinate people against smallpox.

[18] **efficacy**—effectiveness.

[19] **perseverance**—steadfast continuation.

[20] **arrayed**—set.

[21] essay—attempt.

[22] **discretion**—judgment.

Shoshone Camp[23] and obtain what information I could with respect to the country. As we had nothing but a little flour and parched meal[24] to eat except the berries with which the Indians furnished us I directed Drewyer and Shields to hunt a few hours and try to kill something, the Indians furnished them with horses and most of their young men also turned out to hunt. I was very much entertained with a view of this indian chase; it was after a herd of about 10 Antelope and about 20 hunters. it lasted about 2 hours and considerable part of the chase in view from my tent. about 1 A.M. the hunters returned had not killed a single Antelope, and their horses foaming with sweat. my hunters returned soon after and had been equally unsuccessfull. I now directed McNeal to make me a little paste with the flour and added some berries to it which I found very palatable.[25]

The means I had of communicating with these people was by way of Drewyer who understood perfectly the common language of **gesticulation**[26] or signs which seeems to be universally understood by all the Nations we have yet seen. it is true that this language is imperfect and liable to error but is much less so than would be expected. the strong parts of the ideas are seldom mistaken.

I now told Cameahwait[27] that I wished him to speak to his people and engage them to go with me tomorrow to the forks of Jeffersons river where our baggage was by this time arrived with another Chief and a large party of whitemen who would wait my return at that place. that I wish them to take with them about 30 spare horses to transport our baggage to this place where we would then remain sometime among them and trade with them

---

[23] The Shoshones are a Native American people.

[24] parched meal—dried corn.

[25] palatable—tasty.

[26] **gesticulation**—gestures; movements of hands, arms, head, and so forth to convey ideas.

[27] Cameahwait—Shoshone chief.

for horses, and finally concert[28] our future plans for getting on to the ocean and of the trade which would be extended to them after our return to our homes. he complyed with my request and made a lengthey **harangue**[29] to his village. he returned in about an hour and a half and informed me that they would be ready to accompany me in the morning, I promised to reward them for their trouble. Drewyer who had had a good view of their horses estimated them at 400. most of them are fine horses. indeed many of them would make a figure on the South side of James River[30] or the land of fine horses. I saw several with spanish brands on them, and some mules which they informed me that they had also obtained from the Spaniards. I also saw a bridle bit of spanish manufactary, and **sundry**[31] other articles which I have no doubt were obtained from the same source. notwithstanding the extreme poverty of those poor people they are very merry they danced again this evening untill midnight. each warrior keep[s] one or more horses tyed by a cord to a stake near his lodge both day and night and are always prepared for action at a moments warning. they fight on horseback altogether. I observe that the large flies are extreemly troublesome to the horses as well as ourselves.

Letter from Meriwether Lewis to Thomas Jefferson
St. Louis, September 23rd, 1806

SIR: It is with pleasure that I announce to you the safe arrival of myself and party at this place on the [blank space in ms.] inst.[32] with our papers and baggage. No accident has deprived us of a single member of our

---

[28] concert—organize.

[29] **harangue**—speech.

[30] make a figure . . . James River—show off well in Virginia.

[31] **sundry**—various.

[32] inst.—abbreviation for *instant*, which following a date means "in the present month."

party since I last wrote you from the Mandans[33] in April, 1805. In obedience to your orders we have penetrated the continent of North America to the Pacific Ocean and sufficiently explored the interior of the country to affirm that we have discovered the most practicable communication which does exist across the continent by means of the **navigable**[34] branches of the Missouri and Columbia Rivers; this is by way of the Missouri to the foot of the rapids five miles below the great falls of that river, a distance of 2572 miles, thence by land, passing the Rocky Mountains to the Kooskooske 340 and from thence by way of the Kooskooske, and the S. E. branch of the Columbia and the latter river to the ocean of 640 miles making a total of 3555 Miles. . . .

We view this passage across the continent as affording immense advantages to the fur trade, but fear that advantages which it offers as a communication for the productions of the East Indias,[35] to the United States and thence to Europe will never be found equal on an extensive scale to that by the way of the Cape of Good Hope.[36] Still we believe that many articles not bulky, brittle, nor of a perishable nature may be conveyed to the U. States by this route with more facility and less expense than that at present practiced. That portion of the continent watered by the Missouri and all its branches from the Cheyenne upwards is richer in beaver and otter than any country on earth, particularly that proportion of its subsidiary streams lying within the Rocky Mountains; . . . Altho' the Columbia does not as much as the Missouri abound in[37] beaver and otter, yet it is by no means **despicable**[38] in this respect and would furnish profitable

---

[33] Mandans—Indian people with whom the expedition wintered in 1804–1805.

[34] **navigable**—capable of being traveled by boats.

[35] East Indias—Asia.

[36] by . . . Good Hope—by traveling around Africa.

[37] abound in—have plenty of.

[38] **despicable**—worthless.

fur trade. In addition to the otter and beaver, considerable quantities of the finest bear of three species affording a great variety of colors, the Tiger cat, several species of fox, the martin and sea otter, might be procured beside the raccoon and some other animals of an inferior class of furs. If the government will only aid even on a limited scale the enterprise of her Citizens, I am convinced that we shall soon derive the benefits of a most **lucrative**[39] trade from this source. And in the course of 10 or 12 years a tour across the continent by this route will be undertaken with as little concern as a voyage across the Atlantic is at present. . . .

I have brought with me several skins of the sea otter, 2 skins of the native sheep of N. America, 5 skins and skeletons complete of the Bighorn or mountain ram, and a skin of the mule deer, besides the skins of several other **quadrupeds**[40] and birds, natives of the country through which we have passed; I have also preserved a pretty extensive collection of plants. . . . have obtained 10 vocabularies, and have also prevailed on the principal chief of the Mandans to accompany me to Washington; he is now with my worthy friend and colleague, Capt. Clark, and myself at this place, in good health and spirits. With respect to the exertions and services rendered by this **estimable**[41] man, Capt. Wm. Clark, on this expedition I cannot say too much. If, sir, any credit be due to the success of the **arduous**[42] enterprise in which we have been engaged, he is equally with myself entitled to the consideration of yourself and that of our common country.

---

[39] **lucrative**—financially profitable.
[40] **quadrupeds**—four-legged animals.
[41] estimable—admirable; praiseworthy.
[42] **arduous**—difficult.

QUESTIONS TO CONSIDER

1. What purposes did Jefferson give for desiring Lewis to gather information about Indians?

2. About what types of plants and animals did Jefferson particularly want the expedition to gather information?

3. Why did Jefferson think it might be wise for the expedition to persuade some Indian chiefs or young people to accompany them?

4. What does Lewis's journal entry indicate about the source of the horses possessed by the Shoshone people?

5. From his letter to Jefferson, in what ways did Lewis feel the expedition's route could be commercially useful?

6. In what ways does Lewis's letter indicate that he carried out Jefferson's instructions?

Colter's Run

BY JOHN BRADBURY

In the wake of Lewis and Clark came the "mountain men," fiercely independent frontiersmen who made a solitary and dangerous living trapping beaver and trading with the Indians. Among the most famous of these was John Colter (1773?–1843). John Bradbury wrote in the early 1800s about Colter, a member of the Lewis and Clark expedition who set off on his own as a fur trapper.

This man came to St. Louis in May, 1810, in a small canoe, from the headwaters of the Missouri, a distance of three thousand miles, which he **traversed**[1] in thirty days. I saw him on his arrival, and received from him an account of his adventures after he had separated from Lewis and Clark's party; one of these, from its **singularity,**[2] I shall relate. On the arrival of the party on the headwaters of the Missouri, Colter, observing an appearance of abundance of beaver being there, he got permission to remain and hunt for some time, which he did in company

[1] **traversed**—crossed.
[2] **singularity**—uniqueness.

with a man of the name of Dixon, who had traversed the immense tract of country from St. Louis to the headwaters of the Missouri alone. Soon after he separated from Dixon, and trapped in company with a hunter named Potts; and aware of the hostility of the Blackfeet Indians, one of whom had been killed by Lewis, they set their traps at night, and took them up early in the morning, remaining concealed during the day. They were examining their traps early one morning, in a creek about six miles from that branch of the Missouri called Jefferson's Fork, and were ascending in a canoe, when they suddenly heard a great noise, resembling the trampling of animals; but they could not **ascertain**[3] the fact, as the high perpendicular banks on each side of the river **impeded**[4] their view. Colter immediately pronounced it to be occasioned[5] by Indians, and advised an instant retreat; but was accused of cowardice by Potts, who insisted that the noise was caused by buffaloes, and they proceeded on. In a few minutes afterwards their doubts were removed, by a party of Indians making their appearance on both sides of the creek, to the amount of five or six hundred, who beckoned them to come ashore. As retreat was now impossible, Colter turned the head of the canoe to the shore; and at the moment of its touching, an Indian seized the rifle belonging to Potts; but Colter, who is a remarkably strong man, immediately retook it, and handed it to Potts, who remained in the canoe, and on receiving it pushed off into the river. He had scarcely quitted the shore when an arrow was shot at him, and he cried out, *"Colter, I am wounded."* Colter remonstrated[4] with him on the folly of attempting to escape, and urged him to come ashore. Instead of

---

[3] **ascertain**—find out definitely.
[4] **impeded**—blocked.
[5] occasioned—caused.
[6] remonstrated—protested.

complying, he instantly levelled his rifle at an Indian, and shot him dead on the spot. This conduct, situated as he was, may appear to have been an act of madness; but it was doubtless the effect of sudden, but sound reasoning; for if taken alive, he must have expected to be tortured to death, according to their custom. He was instantly pierced with arrows so numerous, that, to use the language of Colter, *"he was made a riddle[7] of."* They now seized Colter, stripped him entirely naked, and began to consult on the manner in which he should be put to death. They were first inclined to set him up as a mark to shoot at; but the chief interfered, and seizing him by the shoulder, asked him if he could run fast? Colter, who had been some time amongst the Kee-kat-sa, or Crow Indians, had in a considerable degree acquired the Blackfoot language, and was also well acquainted with Indian customs. He knew that he had now to run for his life, with the dreadful odds of five or six hundred against him, and those armed Indians; therefore cunningly replied that he was a very bad runner, although he was considered by the hunters as remarkably swift. The chief now commanded the party to remain stationary, and led Colter out on the prairie three or four hundred yards, and released him, bidding him *to save himself if he could.* At that instant the horrid war whoop sounded in the ears of poor Colter, who, urged with the hope of preserving life, ran with a speed at which he was himself surprised. He proceeded towards the Jefferson Fork, having to traverse a plain six miles in breadth, abounding with the prickly pear, on which he was every instant treading with his naked feet. He ran nearly half across the plain before he ventured to look over his shoulder, when he perceived that the Indians were very scattered, and that he had gained ground to a considerable distance from the main body; but one Indian, who

---

[7] *riddle*—sieve; device full of holes.

carried a spear, was much before all the rest, and not more than a hundred yards from him. A faint gleam of hope now cheered the heart of Colter: he derived confidence from belief that escape was within the bounds of possibility; but that confidence was nearly being fatal to him, for he exerted himself to such a degree, that the blood gushed from his nostrils, and soon almost covered the fore part of his body. He had now arrived within a mile of the river, when he distinctly heard the appalling sound of footsteps behind him, and every instant expected to feel the spear of his pursuer. Again he turned his head, and saw the savage not twenty yards from him. Determined if possible to avoid the expected blow, he suddenly stopped, turned round, and spread out his arms. The Indian, surprised by the suddenness of the action, and perhaps at the bloody appearance of Colter, also attempted to stop; but exhausted with running, he fell whilst endeavoring to throw his spear, which stuck in the ground, and broke in his hand. Colter instantly snatched up the pointed part, with which he pinned him to the earth, and then continued his flight. The foremost of the Indians, on arriving at the place, stopped till others came up to join them, when they set up a hideous yell. Every moment of this time was improved by Colter, who, although fainting and exhausted, succeeded in gaining the skirting of the cottonwood trees, on the borders of the fork, through which he ran, and plunged into the river. Fortunately for him, a little below this place there was an island, against the upper point of which a raft of drift timber had lodged. He dived under the raft, and after several efforts, got his head above water amongst the trunks of trees, covered over with smaller wood to the depth of several feet. Scarcely had he secured himself, when the Indians arrived on the river, screeching and yelling, as Colter expressed it, "like so many devils." They were frequently on the raft during the day, and were seen through the chinks[8] by Colter, who was congratulating himself on his escape, until the idea arose that they might set the raft on fire. In horrible suspense he remained until night, when hearing no more of the Indians, he dived from under the raft, and swam silently down the river to a considerable distance, when he landed, and travelled all night. Although happy in having escaped from the Indians, his situation was still dreadful: he was completely naked, under a burning sun; the soles of his feet were entirely filled with the thorns of the prickly pear; he was hungry, and had no means of killing game, although he saw abundance around him, and was at least seven days journey from Lisa's Fort, on the Bighorn branch of the Roche Jaune River. These were circumstances under which almost any man but an American hunter would have despaired. He arrived at the fort in seven days, having subsisted on a root much esteemed by the Indians of the Missouri, now known by naturalists as *psoralea esculenta*.[9]

---

[8] chinks—narrow gaps (here, between the tree trunks).
[9] *psoralea esculenta*—also called breadroot, or, by the French trappers, *pomme blanche* ("white apple").

QUESTIONS TO CONSIDER

1. According to Bradbury's account of Colter, why were the Blackfeet angry at the whites?

2. In Bradbury's view, why did Colter's companion Potts shoot one of the Indians?

3. What qualities of the mountain men are reflected in this episode?

Living with the Indians

BY JAMES P. BECKWOURTH

Living in the wilderness, the mountain men adopted Indian dress and habits and frequently married Indian women. One account of living with the Indians comes from the autobiography of mountain man James P. Beckwourth (1798–1867?). The son of a white man and an African-American woman, Beckwourth went west with a fur-trading expedition in 1822 and spent the next quarter century in the Rocky Mountains.

The same evening Captain Bridger[1] and myself started out with our traps, intending to be gone three or four days. We followed up a small stream until it forked, when Bridger proposed that I should take one fork and he the other, and the one who had set his traps first should cross the hill which separated the two streams and rejoin the other. Thus we parted, expecting to meet

---

[1] Captain Bridger—Jim Bridger (1804–1881), famous fur trapper and mountain man.

again in a few hours. I continued my course up the stream in pursuit of beaver villages until I found myself among an innumerable drove of horses, and I could plainly see they were not wild ones.

The horses were guarded by several of their Indian owners, or horse-guards, as they term them, who had discovered me long before I saw them. I could hear their signals to each other, and in a few moments I was surrounded by them, and escape was impossible. I resigned myself to my fate: if they were enemies, I knew they could kill me but once, and to attempt to defend myself would entail[2] **inevitable**[3] death. I took the chances between death and mercy; I surrendered my gun, traps, and what else I had, and was marched to camp under a strong escort of horse-guards. I felt very sure that my guards were Crows,[4] therefore I did not feel greatly alarmed at my situation. On arriving at their village, I was ushered into the chief's lodge, where there were several old men and women, whom I conceived to be members of the family. My capture was known throughout the village in five minutes, and hundreds gathered around the lodge to get a sight of the prisoner. In the crowd were some who had talked to Greenwood[5] a few weeks before. They at once exclaimed, "That is the lost Crow, the great brave who has killed so many of our enemies. He is our brother."

This threw the whole village in commotion; old and young were impatient to obtain a sight of the "great brave." Orders were immediately given to summon all the old women taken by the Shi-ans[6] at the time of their captivity so many winters past, who had suffered the

---

[2] entail—bring about.

[3] **inevitable**—unavoidable.

[4] Crows—Plains Indian people generally friendly to the whites.

[5] Greenwood—companion of Beckwourth's who had told the Crows that Beckwourth was a Crow who had been captured as a child by the Cheyenne.

[6] Shi-ans—Cheyennes, a Plains Indian people.

loss of a son at that time. The lodge was cleared for the examining committee and the old women, breathless with excitement, their eyes wild and protruding, and their nostrils **dilated**,[7] arrived in squads, until the lodge was filled to overflowing. I believe never was mortal gazed at with such intense and sustained interest as I was on that occasion. Arms and legs were critically scrutinized. My face next passed the ordeal; my neck, back, breast, and all parts of my body, even down to my feet, which did not escape the examination of the anxious matrons, in their endeavors to discover some mark or peculiarity whereby to recognize their brave son.

At length one old woman, after having scanned my **visage**[8] with the utmost intentness, came forward and said "If this is my son, he has a mole over one of his eyes."

My eyelids were immediately pulled down to the utmost stretch of their elasticity, when, sure enough, she discovered a mole just over my left eye!

"Then, and oh then!" such shouts of joy as were uttered by that honest-hearted woman were seldom before heard, while all in the crowd took part in her rejoicing. It was uncultivated joy, but not the less heartfelt and intense. It was a joy which a mother can only experience when she recovers a son whom she had supposed dead in his earliest days. She has mourned him silently through weary nights and busy days for the long space of twenty years; suddenly he presents himself before her in robust manhood, graced with the highest name an Indian can appreciate. It is but nature, either in the savage breast or civilized, that hails such a return with overwhelming joy, and feels mother's undying affection awakened beyond all control.

---

[7] **dilated**—widened.

[8] **visage**—face.

All the other claimants resigning their pretensions,[9] I was fairly carried along by the excited crowd to the lodge of the "Big Bowl," who was my father. The news of my having proved to be the son of Mrs. Big Bowl flew through the village with the speed of lightning, and, on my arrival at the paternal lodge, I found it filled with all degrees of newly-discovered relatives, who welcomed me nearly to death. They seized me in their arms and hugged me, and my face positively burned with the enraptured kisses of my numerous fair sisters, with a long host of cousins, aunts, and other more remote kindred. All these welcoming ladies as firmly believed in my identity with the lost one as they believed in the existence of the Great Spirit.

My father knew me to be his son; told all the Crows that the dead was alive again, and the lost one was found. He knew it was fact; Greenwood had said so, and the words of Greenwood were true; his tongue was not crooked—he would not lie. He also had told him that his son was a great brave among the white men; that his arm was strong; that the Black Feet **quailed**[10] before his rifle and battle-axe; that his lodge was full of their scalps which his knife had taken; that they must rally around me to support and protect me; and that his long-lost son would be a strong breastwork[11] to their nation, and he would teach them how to defeat their enemies.

They all promised that they would do as his words had indicated.

My unmarried sisters were four in number, very pretty, intelligent young women. They, as soon as the departure of the crowd would admit, took off my old leggins, and moccasins, and other garments, and supplied their place with new ones, most beautifully

---

[9] pretensions—claims.
[10] **quailed**—shrank back in fear; cowered.
[11] breastwork—defense.

ornamented according to their very last fashion. My sisters were very ingenious in such work, and they wellnigh[12] quarreled among themselves for the privilege of dressing me. When my toilet[13] was finished to their satisfaction, I could compare in elegance with the most popular warrior of the tribe when in full costume. They also prepared me a bed, not so high as Haman's gallows[14] certainly, but just as high as the lodge would admit. This was also a token of their esteem and sisterly affection.

While conversing to the extent of my ability with my father in the evening, and affording him full information respecting the white people, their great cities, their numbers, their power, their **opulence**,[15] he suddenly demanded of me if I wanted a wife; thinking, no doubt, that, if he got me married, I should lose all discontent, and forgo any wish of returning to the whites.

I assented, of course.

"Very well," said he, "you shall have a pretty wife and a good one."

Away he strode to the lodge of one of the greatest braves, and asked one of his daughters of him to bestow upon his son, who the chief must have heard was also a great brave. The consent of the parent was readily given. The name of my prospective father-in-law was Black-lodge. He had three very pretty daughters, whose names were Still-water, Blackfish, and Three-roads.

Even the untutored daughters of the wild woods need a little time to prepare for such an important event, but long and tedious courtships are unknown among them.

The ensuing day the three daughters were brought to my father's lodge by their father, and I was requested

---

[12] wellnigh—nearly.

[13] toilet—grooming.

[14] In the Bible, Haman is a Persian prince who is hanged for plotting to destroy the Jews.

[15] **opulence**—wealth.

to take my choice. "Still-water" was the eldest, and I liked her name; if it was emblematic of her disposition,[16] she was the woman I should prefer. "Still-water," accordingly, was my choice. They were all superbly attired in garments which must have cost them months of labor, which garments the young women ever keep in readiness against such an interesting occasion as the present.

The acceptance of my wife was the completion of the ceremony, and I was again a married man, as sacredly in their eyes as if the Holy Christian Church had fastened the **irrevocable**[17] knot upon us.

Among the Indians, the daughter receives no patrimony[18] on her wedding-day, and her mother and father never pass a word with the son-in-law after—a custom religiously observed among them, though for what reason I never learned. The other relatives are under no such restraint.

My brothers made me a present of twenty as fine horses as any in the nation—all trained war-horses. I was also presented with all the arms and instruments requisite for an Indian campaign.

My wife's deportment[19] coincided with her name; she would have reflected honor upon many a civilized household. She was affectionate, obedient, gentle, cheerful, and, apparently, quite happy. No domestic thunder-storms, no curtain-lectures[20] ever disturbed the serenity of our connubial[21] lodge. I speedily formed acquaintance with all my immediate neighbors, and the Morning Star (which was the name conferred upon me on my recognition as the lost son) was soon a companion to all the young warriors in the village. No power on

---

[16] emblematic of her disposition—symbolic of her personality, that is, if she was quiet.

[17] **irrevocable**—unalterable.

[18] patrimony—property from her father, that is, a dowry.

[19] deportment—behavior.

[20] curtain-lectures—private scoldings; in reference to bed curtains.

[21] connubial—relating to marriage.

earth could have shaken their faith in my positive identity with the lost son. Nature seemed to prompt the old woman to recognize me as her missing child, and all my new relatives placed implicit faith in the genuineness of her discovery. Greenwood had spoken it, "and his tongue was not crooked." What could I do under the circumstances? Even if I should deny my Crow origin, they would not believe me. How could I dash with an unwelcome and incredible explanation all the joy that had been manifested on my return—the cordial welcome, the rapturous embraces of those who hailed me as a son and a brother, the exuberant joy of the whole nation for the return of a long-lost Crow, who, stolen when a child, had returned in the strength of maturity, graced with the name of a great brave, and the generous strife I had occasioned in their endeavors to accord me the warmest welcome? I could not find it in my heart to undeceive these unsuspecting people and tear myself away from their untutored caresses.

Thus I commenced my Indian life with the Crows. I said to myself, "I can trap in their streams unmolested, and derive more profit under their protection than if among my own men, exposed incessantly to assassination and alarm." I therefore resolved to abide with them, to guard my secret, to do my best in their company, and in assisting them to subdue their enemies.

QUESTIONS TO CONSIDER

1. Why did the Crows believe that Beckwourth was a member of their tribe who had been kidnapped by the Cheyenne?

2. Why did Beckwourth let the Crows believe he was one of their people?

3. What attitude in general did Beckwourth seem to have toward the Indians?

Mountain Jim

BY ISABELLA BIRD

The heyday of the mountain men was the 1820s and 1830s. By the 1840s it was largely over, due to the increase of settlement in the West and a decline in the popularity of beaver hats. This is reflected in an account by Isabella Bird (1831–1904), an English traveler who rode through the Rocky Mountains in late 1873 and described her meeting with the trapper and scout "Mountain Jim," a type of man "for whom there is now no room" in the West.

A very pretty mare, hobbled, was feeding; a collie dog barked at us, and among the scrub, not far from the track, there was a rude, black log cabin, as rough as it could be to be a shelter at all, with smoke coming out of the roof and window. We diverged[1] towards it; it mattered not that it was the home, or rather den, of a notorious "ruffian" and "desperado." One of my companions had disappeared hours before, the remaining one was a town-bred youth. I longed to speak to some one who loved the mountains. I called the hut a *den*—it

---

[1] diverged—went off.

looked like the den of a wild beast. The big dog lay outside it in a threatening attitude and growled. The mud roof was covered with lynx, beaver, and other furs laid out to dry, beaver paws were pinned out on the logs, a part of the carcass of a deer hung at one end of the cabin, a skinned beaver lay in front of a heap of peltry[2] just within the door, and antlers of deer, old horseshoes, and offal[3] of many animals, lay about the den.

Roused by the growling of the dog, his owner came out, a broad, thickset man, about the middle height, with an old cap on his head, and wearing a grey hunting suit much the worse for wear (almost falling to pieces, in fact), a digger's scarf knotted round his waist, a knife in his belt, and "a bosom friend," a revolver, sticking out of the breast pocket of his coat; his feet, which were very small, were bare, except for some **dilapidated**[4] moccasins made of horse hide. The marvel was how his clothes hung together, and on him. The scarf round his waist must have had something to do with it. His face was remarkable. He is a man about forty-five, and must have been strikingly handsome. He has large grey-blue eyes, deeply set, with well-marked eyebrows, a handsome aquiline[5] nose, and a very handsome mouth. His face was smooth shaven except for a dense mustache and imperial.[6] Tawny hair, in thin uncared-for curls, fell from under his hunter's cap and over his collar. One eye was entirely gone, and the loss made one side of the face repulsive, while the other might have been modeled in marble. "Desperado" was written in large letters all over him. I almost repented of having sought his acquaintance. His first impulse was to swear at the dog, but on seeing a lady he contented himself with kicking him,

---

[2] peltry—skins.

[3] offal—remains of butchered animals.

[4] **dilapidated**—worn-out.

[5] aquiline—curved.

[6] imperial—pointed beard.

and coming to me he raised his cap, showing as he did so a magnificently-formed brow and head, and in a cultured tone of voice asked if there were anything he could do for me? I asked for some water, and he brought some in a battered tin, gracefully apologizing for not having anything more presentable. We entered into conversation, and as he spoke I forgot both his reputation and appearance, for his manner was that of a chivalrous gentleman, his accent refined, and his language easy and elegant. I inquired about some beavers' paws which were drying, and in a moment they hung on the horn of my saddle. Apropos of[7] the wild animals of the region, he told me that the loss of his eye was owing to a recent encounter with a grizzly bear, which, after giving him a death hug, tearing him all over, breaking his arm and scratching out his eye, had left him for dead. As we rode away, for the sun was sinking, he said, courteously, "You are not an American. I know from your voice that you are a countrywoman of mine. I hope you will allow me the pleasure of calling on you."

This man, known through the Territories and beyond them as "Rocky Mountain Jim," or, more briefly, as "Mountain Jim," is one of the famous scouts of the Plains, and is the original of some daring portraits in fiction concerning Indian Frontier warfare. So far as I have at present heard, he is a man for whom there is now no room, for the time for blows and blood in this part of Colorado is past, and the fame of many daring exploits is **sullied**[8] by crimes which are not easily forgiven here. He now has a "squatter's claim," but makes his living as a trapper, and is a complete child of the mountains. Of his genius and chivalry to women there does not appear to be any doubt; but he is a desperate character, and is subject to "ugly fits," when people think it best to avoid

---

[7] Apropos of—with reference to.
[8] **sullied**—stained.

him. It is here regarded as an evil that he has located himself at the mouth of the only entrance to the park, for he is dangerous with his pistols, and it would be safer if he were not here. His besetting[9] sin is indicated in the verdict pronounced on him by my host: "When he's sober Jim's a perfect gentleman; but when he's had liquor he's the most awful ruffian in Colorado."

---

[9] besetting—ever-present.

QUESTIONS TO CONSIDER

1. What contradictions existed in the appearance and character of Mountain Jim?

2. Why was Mountain Jim "a man for whom there is now no room" in the West?

3. If you were to judge by Mountain Jim, what were the virtues and failings of the mountain men as a group?

Encountering the Wilderness

▲

Painted by Thomas Moran (1837–1926), *Grand Canyon of the Yellowstone* presents the landscape of the West at its most awe inspiring.

In the early 1830s, Swiss artist Karl Bodmer (1809–1893) traveled throughout the Great Plains recording the lives of the American Indians he encountered. Here he depicts the interior of a Mandan lodge.

▼

▲

This portrait of a Blackfoot chief by American painter George Catlin (1796–1872) is among hundreds of images he created recording Native Americans and their culture.

▲

This lithograph of Fort Laramie, a converted fur-trading post located where the Laramie River meets the North Platte, comes from explorer John C. Frémont's report of his expeditions of 1842 and 1843–1844.

▲

Karl Bodmer's image shows the Assiniboin breaking camp to leave Fort Union,
a post near the present border between Montana and North Dakota.

Establishing
Communities

Spanish California

BY GUADALUPE VALLEJO

California had been part of New Spain since the 1500s, but not until the mid-1700s, when Russians from Alaska began moving south, did the Spanish take serious steps to colonize this territory. Between 1769 and 1823, a series of 21 missions were established by Franciscan monks under the leadership of Junipero Sera (1713–1784). After Mexico became independent of Spain in 1821, California became a Mexican province and remained so until 1848, when it was ceded to the United States. In a magazine article published in 1890, Guadalupe Vallejo (died 1904) presented an affectionate picture of life on the missions and ranches during the period when the Spanish and Mexicans governed the region known as Alta ("Upper") California.

It seems to me that there never was a more peaceful or happy people on the face of the earth than the Spanish, Mexican, and Indian population of Alta California before the American conquest. We were the pioneers of the Pacific coast, building towns and Missions while General Washington was carrying on the war of the Revolution, and we often talk together of the days when a few hundred large Spanish ranches and mission tracts occupied the whole country from the Pacific to the San Joaquin. No class of American citizens is more loyal than the Spanish Californians, but we shall always be especially proud of the traditions and memories of the long **pastoral**[1] age before 1840. Indeed, our social life still tends to keep alive a spirit of love for the simple, homely, outdoor life of our Spanish ancestors on this coast, and we try, as best we may, to honor the founders of our ancient families, and the saints and heroes of our history since the days when Father Junipero Serra planted the cross at Monterey. . . .

The Jesuit Missions established in Lower California,[2] at Loreto and other places, were followed by Franciscan Missions in Alta California, with presidios[3] for the soldiers, adjacent pueblos, or towns, and the granting of large tracts of land to settlers. By 1782 there were nine flourishing Missions in Alta California—San Francisco, Santa Clara, San Carlos, San Antonio, San Luis Obispo, San Buenaventura, San Gabriel, San Juan, and San Diego. Governor Fajés added Santa Barbara and Purissima, and by 1790 there were more than 7,000 Indian converts in the various missions. By 1800 about forty Franciscan fathers were at work in Alta California, six of whom had been among the pioneers of twenty and twenty-five years before, and they had established seven new Missions—San José, San Miguel, Soledad, San Fernando, Santa Cruz, San Juan Bautista, and San Luis Rey. . . .

No one need suppose that the Spanish pioneers of California suffered many hardships or privations, although it was a new country. They came slowly, and were well prepared to become settlers. All that was necessary for the maintenance and enjoyment of life

---

[1] **pastoral**—simple; rustic.

[2] Lower California—the peninsula of Baja California, part of Mexico.

[3] presidios—forts.

according to the simple and healthful standards of those days was brought with them. They had seeds, trees, vines, cattle, household goods, and servants, and in a few years their orchards yielded abundantly and their gardens were full of vegetables. Poultry was raised by the Indians, and sold very cheaply; a fat capon[4] cost only twelve and a half cents. Beef and mutton were to be had for the killing, and wild game was very abundant. At many of the missions there were large flocks of tame pigeons. At the Mission San José the fathers' doves consumed a cental[5] of wheat daily, besides what they gathered in the village. The doves were of many colors, and they made a beautiful appearance on the red tiles of the church and the tops of the dark garden walls.

The houses of the Spanish people were built of adobe,[6] and were roofed with red tiles. They were very comfortable, cool in summer and warm in winter. The clay used to make the bricks was dark brown, not white or yellow, as the adobes in Rio Grande region and in part of Mexico. Cut straw was mixed with the clay, and trodden together by the Indians. When the bricks were laid, they were set in clay as mortar, and sometimes small pebbles from the brooks were mixed with the mortar to make bands across the house. All the timber of the floors, the rafters and crossbeams, the doorways, and the window lintels[7] were "built in" as the house was carried up.[8] After the house was roofed it was usually plastered inside and out to protect it against the weather and make it more comfortable. A great deal of trouble was often taken to obtain stone for the doorsteps, and curious rocks were sometimes brought many miles for this purpose, or for gate-posts in front of the dwelling.

---

[4] capon—chicken.

[5] a cental—100 pounds.

[6] adobe—clay or mud brick.

[7] lintels—frames.

[8] carried up—built.

The Indian houses were never more than one story high, also of adobe, but much smaller and with thinner walls. The inmates[9] covered the earthen floors in part with coarse mats woven of tules,[10] on which they slept. The missions, as fast as possible, provided them with blankets, which were woven under the fathers' personal supervision, for home use and for sale. They were also taught to weave a coarse serge[11] for clothing.

It was between 1792 and 1795, as I have heard, that the governor brought a number of artisans from Mexico, and every mission wanted them, but there were not enough to go around. There were masons, millwrights, tanners, shoemakers, saddlers, potters, a ribbon maker, and several weavers. The blankets and the coarse cloth I have spoken of were first woven in the southern missions, San Gabriel, San Juan Capistrano, and others. About 1797 cotton cloth was also made in a few cases, and the cotton plant was found to grow very well. Hemp was woven at Monterey. Pottery was made at Mission Dolores, San Francisco. Soap was made in 1798, and afterwards at all the missions and on many large ranches. The settlers themselves were obliged to learn trades and teach them to their servants, so that an educated young gentleman was well skilled in arts and handicrafts. He could ride, of course, as well as the best cowboy of the Southwest, and with more grace; and he could throw the lasso so expertly that I never heard of any American who was able to equal it. He could also make pottery, and bricks, burn lime, tan hides, cut out and put together a pair of shoes, make candles, roll cigars and do a great number of things that belong to different trades. . . .

---

[9] **inmates**—inhabitants.
[10] tules—tall grasses; reeds.
[11] serge—woolen cloth.

Indian alcaldes[12] were appointed in the mission towns to maintain order. Their duty was that of police officers; they were dressed better than the others, and wore shoes and stockings, which newly appointed officers dispensed with as often as possible, choosing to go barefoot, or with stockings only. When a vacancy in the office occurred the Indians themselves were asked which one they preferred of several suggested by the priest. The Mission San José had about five thousand Indian converts at the time of its greatest prosperity, and a number of Indian alcaldes were needed there. The alcaldes of the Spanish people in the pueblos were more like local judges, and were appointed by the governor. . . .

It was the custom at all the missions, during the rules of the Franciscan missionaries, to keep the young unmarried Indians separate. The young girls and the young widows at the Mission San José occupied a large adobe building, with a yard behind it, enclosed by high adobe walls. In this yard some trees were planted, and a zanja, or water-ditch, supplied a large bathing-pond. The women were kept busy at various occupations, in the building, under the trees, or on the wide porch; they were taught spinning, knitting, the weaving of Indian baskets from grasses, willow rods, and roots, and more, especially plain sewing. The treatment and occupation of the unmarried women was similar at the other missions. When **heathen**[13] Indian women came in, or were brought by their friends, or by the soldiers, they were put in these houses, and under the charge of older women, who taught them what to do.

The women, thus separated from the men, could only be courted from without through the upper windows facing on the narrow village street. These windows were about two feet square, crossed by iron

---

[12] alcaldes—officials.

[13] **heathen**—not Christian.

bars, and perhaps three feet deep, as the adobe walls were very thick. The rules were not more strict, however, than still prevail in some of the Spanish-American countries in much higher classes, socially, than these uneducated Indians belonged to; in fact, the rules were adopted by the fathers from Mexican models. After an Indian, in his hours of freedom from toil, had declared his affection by a sufficiently long attendance upon a certain window, it was the duty of the woman to tell the father missionary and to declare her decision. If this was favorable, the young man was asked if he was willing to contract marriage with the young woman who had confessed her preference. Sometimes there were several rival suitors, but it was never known that any trouble occurred. After marriage, the couple were conducted to their home, a hut built for them among the other Indian houses in the village near the mission.

The Indian mothers were frequently told about the proper care of children, and cleanliness of the person was strongly inculcated.[14] In fact, the mission Indians, large and small, were wonderfully clean, their faces and hair fairly shining with soap and water. In several cases where an Indian woman was so **slovenly**[15] and neglectful of her infant that it died she was punished by being compelled to carry in her arms in church, and at all meals and public assemblies, a log of wood about the size of a nine-months'-old child. This was a very effectual punishment, for the Indian women are naturally most affectionate creatures, and in every case they soon began to suffer greatly, and others with them, so that once a whole Indian village begged the father in charge to forgive the poor woman.

The padres[16] always had a school for the Indian boys. My mother has a novena, or "nine-days' devotion

---

[14] inculcated—taught through repeated lessons.
[15] **slovenly**—careless.
[16] padres—priests.

book" copied for her by one of the Indian pupils at the Mission San José early in the nineteenth century. The handwriting is very neat and plain, and would be a credit to anyone. Many young Indians had good voices, and these were selected with great care to be trained in singing for the church choir. It was thought such an honor to sing in church that the Indian families were all very anxious to be represented. Some were taught to play on the violin and other stringed instruments. . . .

In the old days every one seemed to live outdoors. There was much gaiety and social life, even though people were widely scattered. We traveled as much as possible on horseback. Only old people or invalids cared to use the slow cart, or carreta. Young men would ride from one ranch to another for parties, and whoever found his horse tired would let him go and catch another. . . .

Family life among the old Spanish pioneers was an affair of dignity and ceremony, but it did not lack in affection. Children were brought up with great respect for their elders. It was the privilege of any elderly person to correct young people by words, or even by whipping them, and it was never told that any one thus **chastised**[17] made a complaint. Each one of the old families taught their children the history of the family, and reverence toward religion. A few books, some in manuscript, were treasured in the household, but children were not allowed to read novels until they were grown. They saw little of other children, except their near relatives, but they had many enjoyments unknown to children now, and they grew up with remarkable strength and healthfulness.

In these days of trade, bustle, and confusion, when many thousands of people live in the Californian valleys, which formerly were occupied by only a few Spanish

---

[17] **chastised**—punished.

families, the quiet and happy domestic life of the past seems like a dream. We, who loved it, often speak of those days, and especially of the duties of the large Spanish households, where so many dependents were to be cared for, and everything was done in a simple and primitive way.

QUESTIONS TO CONSIDER

1. How did Vallejo characterize the life of the first Spanish settlers in California?

2. How do you think this account might have differed if it had been written by one of the Indians living at a mission?

3. How would you describe the ideal of the gentleman as it existed in Spanish California?

4. How much power did women exercise in the courtship conducted by the mission Indians?

5. In early California, what was the attitude toward the elderly? Toward the young?

Early Texas

BY FRANCES COOK LIPSCOMB VAN ZANDT

During hundreds of years of Spanish rule, only a few thousand Mexicans settled in what is now Texas. In the 1820s, the Mexican government invited Americans to come to Texas, and these Anglo newcomers soon outnumbered the earlier Mexican settlers, or Tejanos. In 1836, Texas rebelled against Mexico, and after battles at the Alamo and San Jacinto, succeeded in becoming independent. The new Republic of Texas chose Sam Houston (1793–1863) as its first president. In 1845, after repeated invitations from Houston, the U.S. government annexed Texas, which became the 28th state in the Union. Among the Americans to settle in the Republic of Texas during its brief existence was Frances Van Zandt.

We started to Texas from Tennessee early in January 1839. My husband, Isaac Van Zandt, was then twenty-five years of age, and I was nearly three years younger. We had two children, Louise and Khleber, aged four and two years, respectively. My husband in the financial crash of 1833 had lost his all in a business venture in Mississippi, and had after that studied law. He had been on a visit to Texas the previous Fall, and had decided to move to the new country. We came down by boat from Memphis to Natchez, where Mr. Van Zandt had to attend to some business. From Natchez, we went up to Red River and then to Natchitoches. Thence we went overland to old Camp Sabine on the East Bank of the River of that name. It was then an abandoned post of perhaps fifty houses. There was good water there and the empty houses made it a convenient and much used stopping place for people going back and forth. We stayed there several months, waiting with as much patience as we could for some money my husband expected from a former partner. This never came and we were exasperatingly poor. Worst of all, my husband who was never very strong was often sick. There I sold my two best dresses, one for two bushels of corn and the other for a bottle of medicine. Everything combined to make our stay at Camp Sabine a period of great anxiety. We finally traded the small amount of furniture we had had shipped to Texas for transportation to Harrison County. . . . Our first house there was an unfinished log cabin of one room. We had two neighbors within a mile of us, but the post office was about fourteen miles away. I was constantly afraid of Indians, but we were never troubled by them. Indeed, I never saw but two after we started to Texas.

It was sometimes necessary for my husband to be away from home, and during his absence I found the neighbors always ready to do anything they could for me. I wish that I could emphasize this feature of our early Texan life. *The spirit of helpfulness and friendly fellowship always prevailed. It was one of the best of the good things of the new country.* We were all strangers together, always willing to lend or borrow, as the case might be. Anything one had was at the disposal of the others. If we had no meat, we felt no hesitancy in going to a neighbor for it. . . . In sickness our neighbors were always ready to do all they could to help. I remember that once Mr. Van

Zandt was called away from home, when his little brother who was then living with us was very sick. He sent for a neighbor man to come and stay with me, and another man came and took our gun and killed a deer, for he knew we needed meat. When not well myself, I was so well cared for by my women neighbors as if they had been my own sisters.

. . . Early in 1842 we moved into the first home that we had owned in Texas. It was one large room with a puncheon floor[1]. . . . It was of logs with boards nailed over the cracks, but it was so open that one day the wind blew the top cover off the bed. It was from this house that we started to Washington,[2] and it was in this cabin (or one similar to it in which we had previously lived) *that the Homestead Law[3] was conceived*. It has been said that "necessity is the mother of invention," and we found frequent **verifications**[4] of this. . . .

. . . When our need for things was pressing, we usually found a way for making them. One time Mr. Van Zandt needed a saddle—he made it, having only a drawing knife from which to fashion the saddle-tree from a dead sassafras tree which he cut down for the purpose. His shoes were gone and he could get no others. He bought some red leather, made a last,[5] and manufactured some very respectable shoes, which he wore to Memphis. . . .

. . . In the Spring of 1840, Mr. Van Zandt went to Mississippi, and was gone about three months. The storm that destroyed Natchez occurred while he was on his way home, and when he was longer in getting back than he expected to be, I feared for several weeks that he had been lost in the storm.

---

[1] puncheon floor—floor made of split logs with one side smoothed.

[2] started to Washington—Frances Van Zandt's husband Isaac was the Republic's ambassador to the United States and helped negotiate annexation.

[3] *Homestead Law*—regulations dealing with grants of public land to settlers.

[4] **verifications**—bits of evidence of the truth.

[5] last—foot-shaped form for making shoes.

His introduction to Texas politics occurred just after his return in June. He was sick in bed with a malarial chill,[6] and a neighbor, Bailey Anderson, came to see him. *Then the best man was sought, and not the strongest party man, for we had just one enemy, Mexico.* Mr. Anderson told my husband that the only way for him to defeat an undesirable aspirant for Congress,[7] was for him (Mr. Van Zandt) to run against him. We were all Texans, ready to shed our blood, if need be, for our independence, and bound together by stronger ties than we had ever known in our old homes. My husband had his license to practice law, and had taken the oath of allegiance to Texas. The six months' residence in the Republic, after this oath was taken, which was necessary to make him eligible for office, had not been passed. Before the election in November, however, this qualification would have been met, so he decided to make the race. He was elected; then re-elected the following year. . . .

While Mr. Van Zandt did not always agree with Mr. Houston's views and plans, their relations were, on the whole, very friendly. My husband supported him for President the next year, and later was appointed by him Minister to the United States. It was in May or June of 1842 that Mr. Van Zandt received the appointment to Washington. I remember that we crossed the Louisiana line the day that the vote was taken that transferred the county seat of Harrison County to Marshall. We traveled in a comfortable carry-all[8] and had a good team. We stopped a few days with relatives in Mississippi, and were about a month in reaching middle Tennessee. We were all dressed in garments made from cloth that I and my Negro woman had made. . . . In the Summer of 1843, Mr. Van Zandt came to Tennessee for us, and we went to

---

[6] malarial chill—fever.

[7] aspirant for Congress—candidate for the Texas Legislature.

[8] carry-all—carriage.

Washington. We had a good carriage, but made the latter part of the journey by public stage, because of an accident to our conveyance.

When Mr. Van Zandt went from Texas to Washington, his instructions were to make no overtures, looking to the annexation of Texas, as such advances had been **repulsed**[9] two or three times previously, feel the public pulse, and find out how the Senate stood in regard to the matter. Then, whenever it seemed certain that a treaty could be made, he was to have instructions from the Texas Government. During 1842–1843 he had worked along this line, and by October, 1843, a sufficient number of Senators had pledged themselves to vote for the treaty to insure its adoption. . . .

Finally, in 1845, annexation was accomplished. I am sure this would have been **consummated**[10] in 1843, had not General Houston withheld instructions from Mr. Van Zandt at the time. . . . I thought then, and I still think, that General Houston was a little **loathe**[11] when the time came to transfer Texas and her independence, and a government all her own, (although she was so sorely beset with difficulties), to the United States where she could but be one among many. I must confess that I had a little of this feeling myself. In the Summer of 1844, Mr. Van Zandt, **chagrined**[12] and disappointed over the failure of the Senate to adopt the treaty (though feeling sure of the ultimate success), and realizing that he had done all that he could do, asked to be recalled.[13] He took the children and me to Louisville, while awaiting his recall, and returned to Washington. When the recall

---

[9] **repulsed**—rejected.

[10] **consummated**—completed; realized.

[11] **loathe**—reluctant.

[12] **chagrined**—made unhappy by failure.

[13] recalled—officially voted out of a public office.

came he rejoined me in Louisville, and we came on to Texas, reaching here in November. Thenceforth, we made Marshall our home. We lived for two years rather outside of the town, but in 1846 we moved to a place nearer in.

QUESTIONS TO CONSIDER

1. What contributed to the problems of the Van Zandt family when they first arrived in Texas?

2. What impression did Frances Van Zandt give of community life in early Texas?

3. How did she feel when the Republic of Texas was finally annexed by the United States?

The Donner Party

BY PATRICK BREEN

In 1846, a wagon train of 200 emigrants, organized by George and Jacob Donner of Illinois, journeyed west to California. At Fort Bridger, in what is now Wyoming, the party divided, with a smaller group of 89 people trying an untested shortcut. Trapped by early, extremely heavy snowfalls in the Sierra Nevada Mountains, this group, including the Donner family, were forced to winter in makeshift cabins. When they were rescued four months later, only 47 had survived—reportedly in some cases by eating the bodies of the dead. Among the survivors were Patrick Breen and his family. Breen kept a diary of the Donner Party's ordeal.

Friday Nov. 20th 1846. Came to this place on the 31st of last month that it snowed. We went on to the pass. The snow so deep we were unable to find the road, when[1] within 3 miles of the summit. Then turned back to this **shanty**[2] on the Lake. Stanton came one day after we arrived here. We again took our teams & wagons &

---

[1] when—even though (we were).

[2] **shanty**—roughly built cabin; shack.

made another unsuccessful attempt to cross in company with Stanton. We returned to the shanty it continuing to snow all the time we were here. We now have killed most part of our cattle having to stay here until next spring & live on poor beef without bread or salt. . . .

Wedsd. [December] 30th. Fine clear morning. Froze hard last night. Charley died last night about 10 Oclock. Had with him in money $1.50 two good looking silver watches one razor 3 boxes caps.[3] Keysburg took them into his possession. Spitzer took his coat & waistcoat, Keysburg all his other little effects gold pin one shirt and tools for shaveing.

Thursday 31st. Last of the year, may we with Gods help spend the coming year better than the past which we purpose[4] to do if Almighty God will deliver us from our present dreadful situation which is our prayer if the will of God sees it fitting for us Amen—morning fair now Cloudy wind E by S for three days past. Freezing hard every night. Looks like another snow storm. Snow Storms are dredful to us. Snow very deep. Crust on the snow.

Satd [February] 6th. It snowed faster last night & today than it has done this winter & still Continues without an intermission. Wind SW. Murphys folks or Keysburgs say they cant eat hides. I wish we had enough of them. Mrs. Eddy very weak.

Sund. 7th. Ceased to snow last [night] after one of the most Severe Storms we experienced this winter. The snow fell about 4 feet deep. I had to shovel the snow off our shanty this morning. It thawed so fast & thawed during the whole storm. To day it is quite pleasant. Wind S.W. Milt here to day says Mrs. Reid has to get a hide from Mrs. Murphy & McCutchins child died 2nd of this month.

Mond 8th. Fine clear morning. Wind S.W. Froze hard last [night]. Spitzer died last night about 3 o'clock. We

---

[3] caps—percussion caps, used to ignite gunpowder in a pistol.

[4] purpose—intend.

will bury him in the snow. Mrs. Eddy died on the night of the 7th.

Tuesd. 9th. Mrs. Murphy here this morning. Pikes child all but dead. Milt at Murphys not able to get out of bed. Keysburg never gets up says he is not able. John went down to-day to bury Mrs. Eddy & child. Heard nothing from Graves for 2 or 3 days. Mrs. Murphy just now going to Graves. Fine morning. Wind S.E. Froze hard last night. Begins to thaw in the Sun.

Wedndd. 10th. Beautiful morning. Wind W: froze hard last night. To day thawing in the Sun. Milt Elliot died last night at Murphys Shanty about 9 Oclock P:M: Mrs. Reid went there this morning to see after his effects. J Denton trying to borrow meat for Graves. Had none to give. They have nothing but hides. All are entirely out of meat but a little we have. Our hides are nearly all eat up with Gods help spring will soon smile upon us.

Tuesd. 23. Froze hard last night. To day fine & thawey has the appearance of spring all but the deep snow. Wind S.S.E. Shot Towser [a dog] to day & dressed his flesh. Mrs Graves came here this morning to borrow meat dog or ox. They think I have meat to spare but I know to the Contrary. They have plenty hides. I live principally on the same.

Wend. 24th. Froze hard last night. To day Cloudy looks like a storm. Wind blows hard from the W. Commenced thawing. There has not any more returned from those who started to cross the Mts.

Thursd. 25th. Froze hard last night. Fine & sunshiny to day. Wind W. Mrs. Murphy says the wolves are about to dig up the dead bodies at her shanty, the nights are too cold to watch them, we hear them howl.

Frid 26th. Froze hard last night. Today clear & warm. Wind S.E. blowing briskly. Marthas jaw swelled with the toothache: hungry times in camp, plenty hides but the folks will not eat them. We eat them with a tolerable good appetite. Thanks be to Almighty God. Amen. Mrs.

Murphy said here yesterday that thought she would Commence on Milt. & eat him. I dont [think] that she has done so yet, it is distressing. The Donners told the California folks that they [would] commence to eat the dead people 4 days ago, if they did not succeed that day or next in finding their cattle then under ten or twelve feet of snow & did not know the spot or near it, I suppose they have done so ere this time.

Satd 27th. Beautiful morning sun shineing brilliantly, wind about S.W. The snow has fell in debth about 5 feet but no thaw but [in] the sun in day time. It freezeing hard every night. Heard some geese fly over last night. Saw none.

Sund. 28th. Froze hard last night. To day fair & sunshine. Wind S.E. 1 solitary Indian passed by yesterday come from the lake had a heavy pack on his back. Gave me 5 or 6 roots resembleing Onions in shape. Taste some like a sweet potatoe, all full of little tough fibres.

Mond. March the 1st to [day] fine & pleasant. Froze hard last night. There has 10 men arrived this morning from bear valley with provisions. We are to start in two or three days & Cash our goods here.

QUESTIONS TO CONSIDER

1. On what food did Breen and his family survive?

2. Based on Breen's account, how did his family cope with its ordeal?

3. How did Breen react to the other emigrants' expressed intentions to eat the bodies of the dead?

The Mormon Migration

BY BRIGHAM YOUNG

The Church of Jesus Christ of Latter-day Saints (commonly known as the Mormons) was founded in New York around 1830 by Joseph Smith (1805–1844). The church grew rapidly, but opposition forced Smith and his followers to move first to Ohio, then to Missouri, and finally to Illinois, where Smith and his brother were murdered by a mob. Once again, the Mormons decide to migrate. In 1847, their new leader Brigham Young (1801–1877) organized and led 5,000 Mormon pioneers across the plains from their winter quarters in Nebraska, into the Rocky Mountains, and finally to the valley of the Great Salt Lake, where they established Salt Lake City. Young recorded the events of Mormon migration in his journal.

Friday. [April 23, 1847] The Pioneer company started about noon, crossed Plum Creek and passed a large corn field, the corn stalks still standing, left Pawnee town, soon crossed Ash Creek twelve feet wide, one foot deep, and proceeded two miles to the place designated for crossing the Loup Fork river. A few attempted to cross with their wagons but owing to the quicksand bed of the river experienced difficulty. Dr. Richards reported that he had rode through the Pawnee town about half a mile west of us and had seen the ruins of about 175 houses or lodges averaging from twenty to sixty feet in diameter, all of which had been burnt to the ground by the Sioux Indians at a time when the Pawnees were absent on their hunting expedition. The town had been partially fortified by an embankment of earth and sods about four feet high, having a ditch on the outside; this place has contained about six thousand souls who have been the terror of the Western tribes. The Pioneer company met and after deliberation concluded to build two rafts about sixteen feet long each to carry over our goods on the morrow.

Saturday. [April 24] The "Revenue Cutter" was brought into requisition[1] and some boated their loads over the river. The horses and cattle were driven back and forth loose across the river to pack the quicksand. Stakes were planted at intervals across the river as a guide for the Teamsters.[2] The brethren continued rowing the boat over the river carrying goods, while the lightly loaded wagons continued crossing at the **ford**,[3] which soon became packed and more solid. One of the rafts floated down the river just before the last team crossed. The Company proceeded four miles and encamped. Prof. O. Pratt took an observation.

Monday. [May 10] Traveled ten miles. Bro. Appleton M Harmon made an odometer attached to the wheel of Wm. Clayton's wagon, enabling bro. Clayton to measure the distances of each day's travel.

---

[1] "Revenue Cutter" . . . requisition—a small boat was put into service.

[2] Teamsters—wagon drivers.

[3] **ford**—shallow place where a river or stream can be waded across.

Saturday. [May 29] I called the camp together and remonstrated with[4] those brethren who were giving way to trifling, dancing, and card playing. I warned them in the name of the Lord against the Spirit which many of the Camp possessed, and called upon them to cease their folly and turn to the Lord their God with full purpose of heart to serve him. The brethren of the Twelve, the High Priests, the Bishops, the Seventies,[5] all covenanted[6] to humble themselves, repent of their follies and remember their former covenants. I then told them who did not belong to the Church that they were not at liberty to introduce cards, dancing, or **iniquity**[7] of any description; but they should be protected in their rights and privileges while they conducted themselves well and did not seek to trample on the Priesthood nor **blaspheme**[8] the name of God. Traveled eight and a half miles. Very heavy rain which commenced at five p.m. and continued during the evening, accompanied by thunder and lightning.

Friday. [June 4] Elders Kimball, Richards and I visited Mr. Bordeaux at the Fort. We paid him $15.00 for the use of the ferryboat. Mr. Bordeaux said that this was the most civil and best behaved company that had ever passed the fort. Dr. Luke Johnson professionally attended several persons in the fort. Robert Crow's company, numbering 17 souls, joined the Pioneer Camp. Traveled 8 1/4 miles.

Tuesday. [June 8] Traveled 15 1/2 miles and encamped. Camped on the "La Boute." Hunters killed two deer and one antelope. Met James H. Greeve, William Tucker, James Woodrie, James Bouvoir, and six

---

[4] remonstrated with—protested to.

[5] brethren of the Twelve . . . the Seventies—Mormon officials.

[6] covenanted—promised.

[7] **iniquity**—evil.

[8] **blaspheme**—speak of God in a disrespectful manner; curse using God's name.

other Frenchmen from whom we learned the Mr. Bridger[9] was located about 300 miles west, that the Mountaineers could ride to Salt Lake from Bridger's in two days and that the Utah country was beautiful.

Sunday. [June 27] Left the Sweetwater river and crossed the South pass of the Rocky Mountains and camped on the Dry Sandy after traveling 15 1/4 miles. Moses Harris, a mountaineer, camped with us; from whom we received some Oregon newspapers and a "California Star" published at Yerba Buena by bro. Sam Brannan. He said the country around Salt Lake was barren and sandy, destitute of timber and vegetation except wild sage.

Monday. [June 28] Traveled 15 1/4 miles. Met Cap. James Bridger who said he was ashamed of Fremont's map[10] of this country. Bridger considered it **imprudent**[11] to bring a large population into the Great Basin[12] until it was **ascertained**[13] that grain could be raised. He said he would give one thousand dollars for a bushel of corn raised in the Basin.

Friday. [July 23; at the site of Salt Lake City] The advance company moved about three miles and encamped; Elder Orson Pratt called the camp together, dedicated the land to the Lord, entreated the blessings on the seeds about to be planted and on the labors of His saints in the valley. The camp was organized for work. Elders W. Richards and Geo. A. Smith **exhorted**[14] the

---

[9] Mr. Bridger—Jim Bridger (1804–1881), famous fur trapper and mountain man.

[10] Fremont's map—John Charles Frémont (1813–1890) was an American soldier who explored much of the West.

[11] **imprudent**—unwise.

[12] Great Basin—desert region between the Rocky and Sierra Nevada mountain ranges.

[13] **ascertained**—made certain; proven.

[14] **exhorted**—strongly urged.

brethren to diligence. 11:30 a.m., the committee appointed reported that 20 rods by 40[15] had been staked off by them on which to plant beans, corn, and buckwheat; soil friable,[16] loam and gravel. About noon, the first furrow was turned over by Wm. Carter. Three plows and one harrow[17] were at work most of the afternoon. At two p.m., a company started to build a dam and cut trenches to convey the water on to the land. At three, thermometer 96 degrees. A company **commenced**[18] mowing the grass and preparing a turnip patch. At six, a thundershower passed over the camp. I ascended and crossed over the Big Mountain, when on its summit I directed Elder Woodruff, who had kindly **tendered**[19] me the use of his carriage, to turn the same half way round so that I could have a view of a portion of Salt Lake valley. The spirit of light rested upon me and hovered over the valley, and I felt that there the Saints would find protection and safety. We descended and encamped at the foot of the Little Mountain.

Wednesday. [July 28] Yesterday, accompanied by the brethren of the Twelve and a few others, I started westward. We crossed the river, Jordan, which is about 6 rods wide and three feet deep, proceeded hence about thirteen miles west to a brackish[20] spring at the point of the mountain where we dined, after which we proceeded a few miles to a point on the Salt Lake shore within a few rods of Black Rock, where the party all bathed. Elders Orson Pratt, Willard Richards, and Geo. A. Smith proceeded three miles further west and entered another valley [Tooele]. Returned to the point of the Mountain and encamped for

---

[15] 20 rods by 40—an area of 330 by 660 feet.

[16] friable—easily crumbled.

[17] harrow—device used to prepare soil for planting.

[18] **commenced**—began.

[19] **tendered**—offered.

[20] brackish—somewhat salty.

the night. Today, proceeded in a south course about ten miles. Saw the course of several springs on the east side of the valley, but found no water on the west side; returned to the ford of the Jordan where we partook of refreshments and several bathed. Returned to encampment. Joseph Hancock and Lewis Barney returned from a two days' tour in the mountains East; they reported an abundance of good timber, principally pine, balsam fir and a little cottonwood; access to the same very difficult. This afternoon, accompanied by Elders Heber C. Kimball, Willard Richards, Orson Pratt, Wilford Woodruff, Geo. A. Smith, Amasa Lyman, Ezra T. Benson, and Thomas Bullock, I designated the site for the Temple block between the forks of City Creek, and on motion of Orson Pratt it was unanimously voted that the Temple be built on the site designated. It was also voted that the city lots be ten by twenty rods, 1 1/4 acres, and that the streets be eight rods wide. Elder Geo. A. Smith proposed to lay out squares for markets and lots for school houses. The brethren assembled this evening on the Temple Square site, and voted to build a Temple and lay out a city at this point. I addressed the brethren on the order of building the city and reviewed the persecutions of the Saints.

Friday. [July 30]. All the brethren met at 8 p.m. when praise to God for the safe return of so many of the battalion[21] was given by shouting Hosanna, Hosanna, Hosanna to God and the Lamb[22] forever and ever, Amen. I preached till 10 p.m.

Saturday. [July 31] A brush bowery[23] of 40 by 28 feet made by the battalion brethren. Col. Markham reported that thirteen plows and three harrows had been stocked

---

[21] battalion—body of Mormon pioneers.

[22] Lamb—Jesus Christ.

[23] brush bowery—shaded area for public gatherings.

during the past week, three lots of ground broken up, one lot of 35 acres planted in corn, oats, buckwheat, potatoes, beans, and garden seed.

QUESTIONS TO CONSIDER

1. How did the Mormons succeed in crossing a river where there was quicksand?

2. What different impressions of the Great Basin country were the Mormons given?

3. How did the Mormon elders lay out Salt Lake City?

A Woman's Trip Across the Plains in 1849

BY CATHERINE HAUN

Between the 1840s and the 1860s, thousands of Americans jour-
neyed to the Far West along one of several overland trails, motivated
by a desire for gold, fertile farmlands, a better climate, or simple
wanderlust. For those who survived accidents, disease, hunger,
thirst, exhaustion, Indian attacks, and other perils, the journey took
six months. Among these migrants were a young bride, Catherine
Haun, and her husband, who traveled from Iowa to the California
gold fields in 1849. Long afterward, Haun dictated an account of
her journey to her daughter.

Early in January of 1849 we first thought of emigrating
to California. It was a period of National hard times and
we being financially involved in our business interests
near Clinton, Iowa, longed to go to the new El Dorado[1]

---

[1] new El Dorado—California. El Dorado was the legendary king of a country
of fabulous wealth.

and "pick up" gold enough with which to return and pay off our debts[2]. . . .

Some half dozen families of our neighborhood joined us and probably about twenty-five persons **constituted**[3] our little band.

Our own party consisted of six men and two women. Mr. Haun, my brother Derrick, Mr. Bowen, three young men to act as drivers, a woman cook and myself. Mr. Haun was chosen Major of the company, and as was the custom in those days, his fellow travelers ever afterwards knew him by this title. Derrick was to look after the packing and unpacking coincident[4] to camping at night, keep tab on the commissary department[5] and, when occasion demanded, lend a "helping hand." The latter service was expected of us all—men and women alike, was very indefinite and might mean anything from building campfires and washing dishes to fighting Indians, holding back a loaded wagon on a down grade or lifting it over boulders when climbing a mountain. . . .

Eight strong oxen and four of the best horses on the farm were selected to draw our four wagons—two of the horses were for the saddle.

Two wagons were filled with merchandise which we hoped to sell at fabulous prices when we should arrive in the "land of gold." The theory of this was good but the practice—well, we never got the goods across the first mountain. Flour ground at our own grist mill and bacon of home-curing filled the large, four-ox wagon while another was loaded with barrels of alcohol. The third wagon contained our household effects and provisions. The former consisted of cooking utensils, two boards nailed together, which was to serve as our dining

---

[2] debts—Catherine Haun and her husband had suffered from the financial panic of 1837.

[3] **constituted**—made up.

[4] coincident—related.

[5] commissary department—group concerned with managing food and other supplies.

table, some bedding and a small tent. We had a very generous supply of provisions. All meats were either dried or salted, and vegetables and fruit were dried, as canned goods were not common sixty years or more ago. For luxuries we carried a gallon each of wild plum and crabapple preserves and blackberry jam. Our groceries were wrapped in India rubber covers and we did not lose any of them—in fact still had some when we reached Sacramento.

The two-horse spring wagon was our bed-room and was driven by the Major—on good stretches of road by myself. A hair mattress, topped off with one of feathers and layed on the floor of the wagon with plenty of bedding made a very comfortable bed after a hard day's travel.

In this wagon we had our trunk of wearing apparel, which consisted of underclothing, a couple of blue checked gingham dresses, several large stout aprons for general wear, one light colored for Sundays, a pink calico sunbonnet and a white one intended for "dress up" days. My feminine vanity had also prompted me to include, in this quasi wedding trousseau,[6] a white cotton dress, a black silk manteaux[7] trimmed very fetchingly with velvet bands and fringe, also a lace scuttle-shaped bonnet having a face wreath of tiny pink rosebuds, and on the side of the crown nestled a cluster of the same flowers. With this marvelous costume I had hoped to "astonish the natives" when I should make my first appearance upon the golden streets of the mining town in which we might locate. Should our dreams of great wealth, acquired over night come true it might be embarrassing not to be prepared with a suitable wardrobe for the wife of a very rich man!

---

[6] quasi wedding trousseau—Haun jokes that the clothes she gathered for the trip are something like (quasi) those assembled by a bride for her wedding.

[7] manteaux—cloak.

When we started from Iowa I wore a dark woolen dress which served me almost constantly during the whole trip. Never without an apron and a three-cornered kerchief, similar to those worn in those days I presented a comfortable, neat appearance. The wool protected me from the sun's rays and penetrating prairie winds. Besides it economized in laundrying which was a matter of no small importance when one considers how limited, and often utterly **wanting**[8] were our "wash day" conveniences. The chief requisite, water, being sometimes brought from miles away.

In the trunk were also a few treasures; a bible, medicines, such as quinine, bluemass,[9] opium, whiskey and hartshorn for snake bites and citric acid—an antidote for scurvy.[10] A little of the acid mixed with sugar and water and a few drops of essence of lemon made a fine substitute for lemonade. Our matches, in a large-mouthed bottle were carefully guarded in this trunk.

The pockets of the canvas walls of the wagon held every day needs and toilet articles, as well as small fire arms. The ready shotgun was suspended from the hickory bows of the wagon camp. A ball of twine, an awl[11] and buckskin strings for mending harness, shoes etc. were invaluable. It was more than three months before we were thoroughly equipped and on April 24th, 1849 we left our comparatively comfortable homes—and the uncomfortable creditors—for the uncertain and dangerous trip, beyond which loomed up, in our mind's eye, castles of shining gold. . . .

At the end of a month we reached Council Bluffs, having only traveled across the state of Iowa, a distance of about 350 miles every mile of which was beautifully

---

[8] **wanting**—lacking.

[9] bluemass—medicine made by grinding mercury and licorice into a powder, used as a laxative.

[10] scurvy—disease caused by a vitamin C deficiency.

[11] awl—small, pointed metal tool for making holes in materials such as leather and wood.

green and well watered. We also had the advantage of camping near farm-houses and the generous supply of bread, butter, eggs and poultry greatly facilitated the cooking. Eggs were 2 1/2 cents a dozen—at our journey's end we paid $1 a piece, that is when we had the dollar. Chickens were worth eight and ten cents a piece. When we reached Sacramento $10 was the ruling price and few to be had at that.

As Council Bluffs was the last settlement on the route we made ready for the final plunge into the wilderness by looking over our wagons and disposing of whatever we could spare. . . .

For the common good each party was "sized up" as it were. People insufficiently provisioned or not supplied with guns and ammunition were not desirable but, on the other hand, wagons too heavily loaded might be a hindrance. Such luxuries as rocking chairs, mirrors, washstands and corner what-nots were generally frowned down upon and when their owners insisted upon carrying them they had to be abandoned before long on the roadside and were appropriated by the Indians who were always eager to get anything that might be discarded.

The canvas covered schooners[12] were supposed to be, as nearly as possible, constructed upon the principle of the "wonderful one-horse shay."[13] It was very essential that the animals be sturdy, whether oxen, mules or horses. Oxen were preferred as they were less liable to stampede or be stolen by Indians and for long hauls held out better and though slower they were steady and in the long run performed the journey in an equally brief time. Besides, in an emergency they could be used as beef. When possible the provisions and ammunition

---

[12] schooners—prairie wagons.

[13] "wonderful one-horse shay"—a marvelous carriage described in a satirical poem by Oliver Wendell Holmes (1809–1894). It "was built in such a logical way/It ran a hundred years to a day"—and then "went to pieces at once."

were protected from water and dust by heavy canvas or rubber sheets.

Good health, and above all, not too large a proportion of women and children was also taken into consideration. The morning starts had to be made early—always before six o'clock—and it would be hard to get children ready by that hour. Later on experience taught the mothers that in order not to delay the trains it was best to allow the smaller children to sleep in the wagons until after several hours of travel when they were taken up for the day.

Our caravan had a good many women and children and although we were probably longer on the journey owing to their presence—they exerted a good influence, as the men did not take such risks with Indians and thereby avoided conflict; were more alert about the care of the teams and seldom had accidents; more attention was paid to cleanliness and sanitation and, lastly but not of less importance, the meals were more regular and better cooked thus preventing much sickness and there was less waste of food.

Among those who formed the personnel of our train were the following families—a wonderful collection of many people with as many different dispositions and characteristics, all recognizing their mutual dependence upon each other and bound together by the single aim of "getting to California."

A regulation "prairie schooner" drawn by four oxen and well filled with suitable supplies, with two pack mules following on behind was the equipment of the Kenna family. There were two men, two women, a lad of fifteen years, a daughter thirteen and their half brother six weeks of age. This baby was our mascot and the youngest member of the company. . . .

One family by the name of Lamore, from Canada, consisted of man, wife and two little girls. They had only a large express wagon drawn by four mules and a meager but well chosen, supply of food and feed. A tent was strapped to one side of the wagon, a roll of bedding to the other side, baggage, bundles, pots, pans and bags of horse feed hung on behind; the effect was really grotesque. As they had already traveled half across the continent, seemed in good shape and were experienced emigrants they passed muster and were accepted. Not encumbered with useless luggage and Mr. Lamore being an expert driver his wagon did not sink into the mud or sand and got over grades and through creeks with comparative ease. He required but little help thus being a desirable member of the train.

Mr. West from Peoria, Ill. had another man, his wife, a son Clay about 20 years of age and his daughter, America, eighteen. Unfortunately Mr. West had gone to the extreme of providing himself with such a heavy wagon and load that they were deemed objectionable as fellow argonauts.[14] After disposing of some of their supplies they were allowed to join us. They had four fine oxen. This wagon often got stalled in bad roads much to the annoyance of all, but as he was a wagon maker and his companion a blacksmith by trade and both were accommodating there were always ready hands to "pry the wheel out of mire." . . .

A mule team from Washington, D.C. was very insufficiently provisioned . . . [by] Southern gentlemen "unused to work. . . ." They deserted the train at Salt Lake as they could not proceed with their equipment and it was easier to embrace Mormonism than to brave the "American Desert."

Much in contrast to these men were four bachelors Messers Wilson, Goodall, Fifield and Martin, who had a wagon drawn by four oxen and two milch[15] cows following behind. The latter gave milk all the way to the

---

[14] argonauts—travelers.

[15] milch—milk-giving.

sink of the Humboldt[16] where they died, having acted as **draught**[17] animals for several weeks after the oxen had perished. Many a cup of milk was given to the children of the train and the mothers tried in every way possible to express their gratitude. When these men lost all their stock and had to abandon their wagon they found that through their generosity they had made many friends. Having cast their bread, or milk, upon the waters it returned, double fold. I remember the evenings' milking was used for supper, but that milked in the morning was put into a high tin churn and the constant jostling that it got all day formed butter and delicious butter-milk by night. We all were glad to swap some of our food for a portion of these delicacies.

After a sufficient number of wagons and people were collected at this **rendezvous**[18] we proceeded to draw up and agree upon a code of general regulations for train government and mutual protection—a necessary precaution when so many were to travel together. Each family was to be independent yet a part of the grand unit and every man was expected to do his individual share of general work and picket duty.

John Brophy was selected as Colonel. He was particularly eligible having served in the Black Hawk War[19] and as much of his life had been spent along the frontier his experience with Indians was quite exceptional.

Each week seven Captains were appointed to serve on "Grand Duty." They were to protect the camps and animals at night. One served each night and in case of danger gave the alarm.

When going into camp the "leader wagon" was turned from the road to the right, the next wagon turned

---

[16] sink of the Humboldt—lake in western Nevada into which the Humboldt River empties.

[17] **draught**—draft, used for pulling loads.

[18] **rendezvous**—meeting place.

[19] Black Hawk War—conflict in 1832 with Sauk and Fox Indians led by Black Hawk (1767–1838).

to the left, the others following close after and always alternating to right and left. In this way a large circle, or corral, was formed within which the tents were pitched and the oxen herded. The horses were picketed[20] near by until bed time when they were tethered to the tongues of the wagons.

While the stock and wagons were being cared for, the tents erected and camp fires started by the side of the wagons outside the corral, the cooks busied themselves preparing the evening meal for the hungry, tired, impatient travelers.

When the camp ground was desirable enough to warrant it we did not travel on the Sabbath.

Although the men were generally busy mending wagons, harness, yokes, shoeing the animals etc., and the women washed clothes, boiled a big mess of beans, to be warmed over for several meals, or perhaps mended clothes or did other household straightening up, all felt somewhat rested on Monday morning, for the change of occupation had been refreshing.

If we had devotional service the minister—pro tem[21]— stood in the center of the corral while we all kept on with our work. There was no disrespect intended but there was little time for leisure or that the weary pilgrim could call his own.

When possible we rested the stock an hour at noon each day; allowing them to graze, if there was anything to graze upon, or in any case they could lie down, which the fagged[22] beasts often preferred to do as they were too tired to eat what we could give them. During the noon hour we refreshed ourselves with cold coffee and a crust of bread. Also a halt of ten minutes each hour was appreciated by all and was never a loss of time.

---

[20] picketed—secured by a rope to a peg driven into the ground.

[21] pro tem—short for pro tempore, Latin phrase meaning "for the time being."

[22] fagged—tired.

However, these **respites**[23] could not always be indulged in as often the toil had to be kept up almost all day and much of the night—because of lack of water. Night work told very seriously upon the stock—they were more worn with one night's travel than they would have been by several day's work, indeed, invariably one or more poor beasts fell by the wayside—a victim of thirst and exhaustion. . . .

During the entire trip Indians were a source of anxiety, we being never sure of their friendship. Secret dread and alert watchfulness seemed always necessary for after we left the prairies they were more treacherous and numerous being in the language of the pioneer trapper: "They wus the most onsartainest vermints alive."

One night after we had retired, some sleeping in blankets upon the ground, some in tents, a few under the wagons and others in the wagons, Colonel Brophy gave the men a practice drill. It was **impromptu**[24] and a surprise. He called: "Indians, Indians!" We were thrown into great confusion and excitement but he was gratified at the promptness and courage with which the men responded. Each immediately seized his gun and made ready for the attack. The women had been instructed to seek shelter in the wagons at such times of danger, but some screamed, others fainted, a few crawled under the wagons and those sleeping in wagons generally followed their husbands out and all of us were nearly paralized with fear. Fortunately, we never had occasion to put into actual use this maneuver, but the drill was quite reassuring and certainly we womenfolk would have acted braver had the alarm ever again been sounded. . . .

The Indian is a financier of no mean ability and invariably comes out A1 in a bargain. Though you may, for the time, congratulate yourself upon your own

---

[23] **respites**—breaks; short intervals of rest or relief.

[24] **impromptu**—not planned in advance.

sagacity,[25] you'll be apt to realize a little later on that you were not quite equal to the shrewd redman[26]—had got the "short end of the deal." One of their "business tricks" was to sell horses or other necessities which were their booty acquired during an attack upon a preceding train. When we were well along in our journey—in the Humboldt Sink—we overtook emigrants one of whom had swapped his watch with the Indians for a yoke of oxen. A few hours afterwards he found that they had been stolen when left to rest while the owners had gone in search of water. The rightful owners established their claim and after a compromise the oxen were joint property. The watch being the profit of the middleman. . . .

It was the fourth of July when we reached the beautiful Laramie River. Its sparkling, pure waters were full of myriads of fish that could be caught with scarcely an effort. It was necessary to build barges to cross the river and during the enforced delay our animals rested and we had one of our periodical "house cleanings." This general systematic re-adjustment always freshened up our wagon train very much, for after a few weeks of travel things got mixed up and untidy and often wagons had to be abandoned if too worn for repairs, and generally one or more animals had died or been stolen.

After dinner that night it was proposed that we celebrate the day and we all heartily join[ed] in. America West was the Goddess of Liberty, Charles Wheeler was orator and Ralph Cushing acted as master of ceremonies. We sang patriotic songs, repeated what little we could of the Declaration of Independence, fired off a gun or two, and gave three cheers for the United States and California Territory in particular!

The young folks decorated themselves in all manner of fanciful and grotesque costumes—Indian characters

---

[25] **sagacity**—wisdom.

[26] redman—term used to describe Native Americans.

being most popular. To the rollicking music of violin and Jew's harp[27] we danced until midnight. There were Indian spectators, all bewildered by the (to them) weird war dance of the Pale Face and possibly they deemed it advisable to sharpen up their arrow heads. During the frolic when the sport was at its height a strange white woman with a little girl in her sheltering embrace rushed into the corral. She was trembling with terror, tottering with hunger. Her clothing was badly torn and her hair disheveled. The child crouched with fear and hid her face within the folds of her mother's tattered skirt. The woman could give no account of her forlorn condition but was only able to sob: "Indians," and "I have nobody nor place to go to." After she had partaken of food and was refreshed by a safe night's rest she recovered and the next day told us that her husband and sister had contracted cholera[28] on account of which her family consisting of husband, brother, sister, herself and two children had stayed behind their train. The sick ones died and while burying the sister the survivors were attacked by Indians, who, as she supposed, killed her brother and little son. She was obliged to flee for her life dragging with her the little five year old daughter.

She had been three days walking back to meet a train. It had been necessary, in order to avoid Indians, to conceal herself behind trees or boulders much of the time and although she had seen a train in the distance before ours she feared passing the Indians that were between the emigrants and herself. She had been obliged to go miles up the Laramie to find a place where she could get across by wading from rock to rock and the swift current had lamed her and bruised her body.

---

[27] Jew's harp—small instrument consisting of a metal frame held between the teeth and a projecting steel tongue that is plucked to produce a soft twanging sound.

[28] cholera—infectious disease that is frequently fatal.

Raw fish that she had caught with her hands and a squirrel that she killed with a stone had been their only food. Our noise and campfire had attracted her and in desperation she braved the Indians around us and trusting to the darkness ventured to enter our camp. Martha, for that was her name, had emigrated from Wisconsin and pleaded with us to send her home; but we had now gone too far on the road to meet returning emigrants, so there was no alternative for her but to accept our protection and continue on to California. When she became calm and somewhat reconciled to so long and uncertain a journey with strangers she made herself useful and loyally cast her lot with us. She assisted me with the cooking for her board; found lodgings with the woman whose husband was a cripple and in return helped the brave woman drive the ox team. Mr. & Mrs. Lamore kept her little girl with their own. . . .

Upon the second day of our resumed travel, still following up the North Platte, Martha spied a deserted wagon some little distance off the road which she recognized as her own. Mr. Bowen went with her to investigate, hoping to find her brother and son. The grave of her sister was still open and her clothing as well as that of her husband, who was in the wagon where he had died, were missing. The **gruesome**[29] sight drove her almost mad. Mr. Bowen and she did not bury the bodies lest they might bring contagion back to us. No trace of either brother or son could be found. All supplies and the horses had been stolen by the Indians.

Cholera was **prevalent**[30] on the plains at this time; the train preceding as well as the one following ours had one or more deaths, but fortunately we had not a single case of the disease. Often several graves together stood as silent proof of smallpox or cholera epidemic. The

---

[29] **gruesome**—shocking; frightful.
[30] **prevalent**—common.

Indians spread the disease among themselves by digging up the bodies of the victims for the clothing. The majority of the Indians were badly pock-marked. . . .

Our only death on the journey occurred in this desert. The Canadian woman, Mrs. Lamore, suddenly sickened and died,[31] leaving her two little girls and grief stricken husband. We halted a day to bury her and the infant that had lived but an hour, in this weird, lonely spot on God's footstool away apparently from everywhere and everybody.

The bodies were wrapped together in a bedcomforter and wound, quite mummyfied with a few yards of string that we made by tying together torn strips of a cotton dress skirt. A passage of the Bible (my own) was read; a prayer offerred and "Nearer, My God to Thee" sung. Owing to the unusual surroundings the ceremony was very impressive. Every heart was touched and eyes full of tears as we lowered the body, coffinless, into the grave. There was no tombstone—why should there be— the poor husband and orphans could never hope to revisit the grave and to the world it was just one of the many hundreds that marked the trail of the argonaut.

---

[31] suddenly . . . died—Mrs. Lamore actually died as a result of childbirth, a fact Haun obscures.

QUESTIONS TO CONSIDER

1. What evidence is there in Haun's account that her wagon train was well organized?

2. What do the California food prices mentioned by Haun indicate about the area's economy during the gold rush?

3. According to Haun, what were the advantages and disadvantages of having large numbers of women and children on a wagon train?

4. What attitude did Haun have toward the Indians?

Gunfight at the O.K. Corral

One of the major problems faced in building community life in the West was maintaining law and order. Law enforcement in frontier boomtowns, such as Tombstone, Arizona, was often left to individuals like Wyatt Earp (1848–1929) and his brothers Virgil and Morgan, who were peace officers, bartenders, and gamblers. The most famous episode of swift and bloody law enforcement in frontier history took place at around 2:30 P.M. on October 26, 1881, a half-block from the rear entrance of the O.K. Corral in Tombstone. On one side were the three Earp brothers and their friend John "Doc" Holliday (1850–1887), a sometime dentist and gambler. Facing them were two pairs of brothers, Ike and Billy Clanton and Tom and Frank McLaury, and their friend Billy Claiborne, all members of a rough crowd known as "the Cowboys." The Earps' expressed purpose was to disarm the Cowboys. It is uncertain who fired first, but when the thirty-second shootout was over, the McLaurys and Billy Clanton were dead, and Morgan and Virgil Earp and Holliday were wounded. An inquest was held, but the judge, a friend of the Earps, dismissed murder charges against them and Holliday. In the following documents, the events are described in a newspaper account and by two witnesses who testified at the inquest.

Account from The Tombstone Epitaph

Stormy as were the early days of Tombstone nothing ever occurred equal to the event of yesterday. Since the retirement of Ben Sippy as marshal and the appointment of V[irgil] W. Earp to fill the vacancy the town has been noted for its quietness and good order. The **fractious**[1] and much dreaded Cowboys when they came to town were upon their good behavior and no unseemly brawls were indulged in, and it was hoped by our citizens that no more such deeds would occur as led to the killing of Marshal White one year ago. This time it struck with its full and awful force upon those who, heretofore, have made the good name of this county a byword and a reproach,[2] instead of upon some officer in the discharge of his duty or a peaceable and unoffending citizen.

Since the arrest of Stilwell and Spence for the robbery of the Bisbee stage, there have been oft repeated threats conveyed to the Earp brothers—Virgil, Wyatt, and Morgan—that the friends of the accused, or in other words the Cowboys, would get even with them for the part they had taken in the pursuit and arrest of Stilwell and Spence. . . .

Sometime Tuesday Ike Clanton came into town and during the evening had some little talk with Doc Holliday and Marshal Earp but nothing to cause either to suspect, further than their general knowledge of the man and the threats that had previously been conveyed to the Marshal, that the gang intended to clean out the Earps. . . . Shortly after this occurrence someone came to the Marshal and told him that the McLaurys had been seen a short time before just below town. Marshal Earp, now knowing what might happen and feeling his responsibility for the peace and order of the city, stayed on duty all night and added to

---

[1] **fractious**—unruly.

[2] byword and a reproach—an object of scorn and blame.

the police force his brother Morgan and Holliday. The night passed without any disturbance whatever and at sunrise he went home and retired to rest and sleep. A short time afterwards one of his brothers came to his house and told him that Clanton was hunting him with threats of shooting him on sight. He discredited[3] the report and did not get out of bed. It was not long before another of his brothers came down, and told him the same thing. Whereupon he got up, dressed and went with his brother Morgan uptown. They walked Allen Street to Fifth, crossed over to Fremont and down to Fourth, where, upon turning up Fourth toward Allen they came upon Clanton with a Winchester rifle in his hand and revolver on his hip. The marshal walked up to him, grabbed the rifle and hit him a blow on his head at the same time, stunning him so that he was able to disarm him without further trouble. He marched Clanton off to the police court, fined Clanton $25 and costs making $27.50 altogether. This occurrence must have been about 1 o'clock in the afternoon.

Inquest Testimony by R. F. Coleman

I was in the O.K. Corral at 2:30 P.M., when I saw the two Clantons and the two McLaury boys in earnest conversation across the street, in Dunbar's corral. I went up the street and notified Sheriff Behan, and told him it was my opinion they meant trouble, and that it was his duty, as Sheriff, to go and disarm them; I told him they had gone to the West End Corral. I then went and saw Marshal Virgil Earp, and notified him to the same effect. I then met Billy Allen, and we walked through the O.K. Corral, about fifty yards behind the Sheriff.

On reaching Freemont street I saw Virgil Earp, Wyatt Earp, Morgan Earp and Doc Holliday, in the center of the street, all armed. I had reached Bauer's meat market;

---

[3] discredited—did not believe.

Johnny Behan had just left the Cowboys, after having a conversation with them. I went along to Fly's photograph gallery, when I heard Virg. Earp say, "Give up your arm; or throw up your arms." There was some reply made by Frank McLaury, but at the same moment there were two shots fired simultaneously by Doc Holliday and Frank McLaury, when the firing became general, over thirty shots being fired.

Tom McLaury fell first, but raised and fired again before he died. Bill Clanton fell next, and raised to fire again when Mr. Fly took his revolver from him. Frank McLaury ran a few rods[5] and fell. Morgan Earp was shot through and fell, Doc Holliday was hit in the left hip, but kept on firing. Virgil Earp was hit in the third or fourth fire in the leg, which staggered him, but he kept up his effective work. Wyatt Earp stood up and fired in rapid succession, as cool as a cucumber, and was not hit. Doc Holliday was as calm as if at target practice and fired rapidly. After the firing was over, Sheriff Behan went up to Wyatt Earp and said, "I'll have to arrest you." Wyatt replied, "I won't be arrested today. I am right here and am not going away. You have deceived me; you told me those men were disarmed. I went to disarm them."

Inquest Testimony by Wesley Fuller

I was going down Allen street, and saw the parties standing on Freemont street and went down the alley to see Billy Clanton, and tell him to get out of town. I saw Billy Clanton, Frank McLaury and Johnny Behan on Freemont street. . . . The Earps and Holliday were on the corner of Fourth and Allen streets when I saw them armed. Virg. Earp had a shotgun, double barreled; the others had six-shooters. I did not go close enough to tell Billy Clanton anything before the difficulty. I saw the Earps through the alley, just as they got there.

---

[5] a few rods—a short distance. A rod equals sixteen and a half feet.

I heard some one say, "Throw up your hands!" Billy Clanton threw up his hands and said, "Don't shoot me; I don't want to fight!" At the same time, the shooting commenced.

I did not see Ike Clanton at that time; I did not see Frank McLaury. The Earp party fired the first shot; two shots were fired right away; they were almost together, I think they were both pistol shots. Both parties then commenced firing rapidly. Billy Clanton staggered and fell at the end of the house. I think five or six shots were fired by the Earp party before Billy Clanton and Frank McLaury commenced shooting. They were the only ones of the Clanton-McLaury party I saw fire. At the time the first shots were fired by the Earp party, Billy Clanton's hands were up level with his head. When firing commenced Frank McLaury was standing by and holding his horse. He was doing nothing. I saw his hands; saw no weapon in them; would have seen it if he had one. The first two shots fired were directed at, and that one shot took effect on, Billy Clanton. I saw he was hit; he put his hand down against his stomach, and wheeled around.

QUESTIONS TO CONSIDER

1. With which side in the gunfight did *The Tombstone Epitaph* appear to sympathize?

2. Why, from these different accounts, is it difficult to figure out what happened? How do they differ?

3. What does this episode tell you about frontier law enforcement?

African Americans in Oklahoma Territory

BY BOOKER T. WASHINGTON

The Civil War ended slavery, but African Americans in the South still struggled with poverty and white racism. Since most African Americans were unable to acquire land in the South, thousands headed west. Many of these migrants went to the Indian Territory, now Oklahoma. By 1890, twenty-eight all-black towns had been established. One of these communities was visited in 1905 by African-American leader Booker T. Washington (1856–1915).

Boley, Oklahoma

Boley, Indian Territory, is the youngest, the most enterprising and in many ways the most interesting of the negro towns in the United States. A rude, bustling, western town, it is a characteristic product of the negro immigration from the South and Middle West into the new lands of what is now the state of Oklahoma.

The large proportions of the northward and west-ward movement of the negro population recall the Kansas exodus of thirty years ago, when within a few months more than forty thousand helpless and **destitute**[1] negroes from the country districts of Arkansas and Mississippi poured into eastern Kansas in search of "bet-ter homes, larger opportunities, and kindlier treatment."

It is a striking evidence of the progress made in thirty years that the present northward and westward movement of the negro people has brought into these new lands, not a helpless and ignorant **horde**[2] of black people, but land-seekers and home-builders, men who have come prepared to build up the country. In the thirty years since the Kansas exodus the southern negroes have learned to build schools, to establish banks and conduct newspapers. They have recovered something of the knack for trade that their foreparents in Africa were famous for. They have learned through their churches and their secret orders the art of corporate and united action. This experience has enabled them to set up and maintain in a raw western community, numbering 2,500, an orderly and self-respecting government.

In the fall of 1905 I spent a week in the Territories of Oklahoma and Indian Territory. During the course of my visit I had an opportunity for the first time to see the three races—the negro, the Indian, and the white man—living side by side, each in sufficient numbers to make their influence felt in the communities of which they were a part, and in the Territory as a whole.

. . . One cannot escape the impression, in traveling through Indian Territory, that the Indians, who own practically all the lands, and until recently had the local government largely in their own hands, are to a very large extent regarded by the white settlers, who are

---

[1] **destitute**—very poor; without resources.

[2] **horde**—large group or crowd.

rapidly filling up the country, as almost a **negligible**[3] quantity. To such an extent is this true that the Constitution of Oklahoma, as I understand it, takes no account of the Indians in drawing its distinctions among the races. For the Constitution there exist only the negro and the white man. The reason seems to be that the Indians have either receded—"gone back," as the saying in that region is—on the advance of the white race, or they have intermarried with and become absorbed with it. Indeed, so rapidly has this intermarriage of the two races gone on, and so great has been the demand for Indian wives, that in some of the Nations, I was informed, the price of marriage licenses has gone as high as $1,000.

The negroes, immigrants to Indian Territory, have not, however, "gone back." One sees them everywhere, working side by side with white men. They have their banks, business enterprises, schools, and churches. There are still, I am told, among the "natives" some negroes who cannot speak the English language, and who have been so thoroughly bred in the customs of the Indians that they have remained among the hills with the tribes by whom they were adopted. But, as a rule, the negro natives do not shun the white man and his civilization, but, on the contrary, rather seek it, and enter, with the negro immigrants, into competition with the white man for its benefits.

This fact was illustrated by another familiar local expression. In reply to my inquiries in regard to the little towns through which we passed, I often had occasion to notice the expression, "Yes, so and so? Well, that is a 'white town.'" Or again, "So and so, that's colored."

I learned upon inquiry that there were a considerable number of communities throughout the Territory where an effort had been made to exclude negro settlers.

---

[3] **negligible**—insignificant.

To this the negroes had replied by starting other communities in which no white man was allowed to live. For instance, the thriving little city of Wilitka, I was informed, was a white man's town until it got the oil mills. Then they needed laborers, and brought in the negroes. There are a number of other little communities—Clairview, Wildcat, Grayson, and Taft—which were sometimes referred to as "colored towns," but I learned that in their cases the expression meant merely that these towns had started as negro communities or that there were large numbers of negroes there, and that negro immigrants were wanted. But among these various communities there was one of which I heard more than the others. This was the town of Boley, where, it is said, no white man has ever let the sun go down upon him.

In 1905, when I visited Indian Territory, Boley was little more than a name. It was started in 1903. At the present time it is a thriving town of 2,500 inhabitants, with two banks, two cotton gins, a newspaper, a hotel, and a "college," the Creek-Seminole College and Agricultural Institute.

There is a story told in regard to the way in which the town of Boley was started, which, even if it is not wholly true as to the details, is at least characteristic, and illustrates the temper of the people in that region.

One spring day, four years ago, a number of gentlemen were discussing, at Wilitka, the race question. The point at issue was the capability of the negro for self-government. One of the gentlemen, who happened to be connected with the Fort Smith Railway, maintained that if the negroes were given a fair chance they would prove themselves as capable of self-government as any other people of the same degree of culture and education. He asserted that they had never had a fair chance. The other gentlemen naturally asserted the contrary. The result of the argument was Boley. Just at that time a number of other town sites were being laid out along the railway which connects Guthrie, Oklahoma, with Fort Smith, Arkansas. It was, it is said, to put the capability of the negro for self-government to the test that in August, 1903, seventy-two miles east of Guthrie, the site of the new negro town was established. It was called Boley, after the man who built that section of the railway. A negro town-site agent, T. M. Haynes, who is at present connected with the Farmers' and Merchants' Bank, was made Town-site Agent, and the purpose to establish a town which should be exclusively controlled by negroes was widely advertised all over the Southwest. . . .

A large proportion of the settlers of Boley are farmers from Texas, Arkansas, and Mississippi. But the desire for western lands has drawn into the community not only farmers, but doctors, lawyers, and craftsmen of all kinds. The fame of the town has also brought, no doubt, a certain proportion of the drifting population. But behind all other attractions of the new colony is the belief that here negroes would find greater opportunities and more freedom of action than they have been able to find in the older communities North and South.

QUESTIONS TO CONSIDER

1. In Washington's view, how did the African-American settlers in Oklahoma differ from earlier migrants?

2. Why had African Americans come to some formerly all-white towns in Oklahoma?

3. Why had the town of Boley been established?

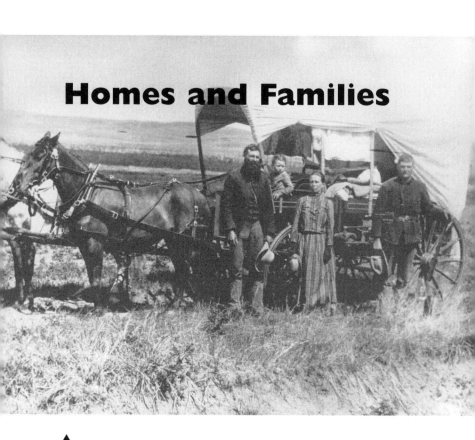

Homes and Families

▲
A family stands beside its wagon on the way to a homestead on the Great Plains in 1886.

▲
One of the emigrants' worst fears on their journeys westward was the possibility of an Indian attack, such as the one in this engraving from 1857.

◀ A group of Mormons journeys to Utah in a caravan of covered wagons around 1879.

▲
Tejon Ranch, where this family was photographed outside its home in 1890, is a community northwest of Los Angeles.

◀ A Nebraska family poses in front of its sod house for Solomon D. Butcher (1856–1927), who took thousands of pictures of pioneer families, mostly his neighbors in Custer County, Nebraska.

▲

Denver, before it became a mining boomtown in the 1870s and 1880s.

▲
The post office and other buildings in Flagstaff, Arizona Territory, around 1899.

Front Street in Portland, Oregon, in 1852.
▼

▲
Los Angeles in the early 1850s.

Making a Living

Mining in California

BY LOUISA CLAPPE

In January 1848, gold was discovered in California, sparking a massive gold rush that drew tens of thousands of people from the United States, South America, Europe, and Asia. The following year, Louisa Clappe (1819–1906) and her husband, a doctor, traveled from Massachusetts to the California gold fields. In 1851 and 1852, she wrote a series of letters to her sister back home, signing herself "Dame Shirley." The Shirley Letters, which were serialized two years later in a California magazine, provide one of the best accounts of the early days of the California gold rush.

Our countrymen are the most discontented of mortals. They are always longing for "big strikes." If a "claim" is paying them a steady income, by which, if they pleased, they could lay up more in a month, than they could accumulate in a year at home, still, they are dissatisfied, and, in most cases, will wander off in search of better "diggings." There are hundreds now pursuing this foolish course, who, if they had stopped where they first "camped," would now have been rich men. Sometimes, a company of these wanderers will find itself upon a bar,[1] where a few pieces of the precious metal lie scattered upon the surface of the ground; of course they immediately "prospect" it, which is accomplished, by "panning out" a few basinsful of the soil. If it "pays," they "claim" the spot, and build their shanties; the news spreads that wonderful "diggings" have been discovered at such a place,—the monte-dealers,[2] those worse than fiends, rush vulture-like upon the scene and erect a round tent, where, in gambling, drinking, swearing and fighting, the *many* reproduce Pandemonium[3] in more than its original horror, while a *few* honestly and industriously commence digging for gold, and lo! as if a fairy's wand had been waved above the bar, a full-grown mining town hath sprung into existence.

But first, let me explain to you the "claiming" system. As there are no State laws upon the subject, each mining community is permitted to make its own. Here, they have decided that no man may "claim" an area of more than forty feet square. This he "stakes off" and puts a notice upon it, to the effect that he "holds" it for mining purposes. If he does not choose to "work it" immediately, he is obliged to renew the notice every ten days; for without this precaution, any other person has a right to "jump it," that is, to take it from him. There are many ways of evading the above law. For instance, an individual can "hold" as many "claims" as he pleases, if he keeps a man at work in each, for this workman represents the original owner. I am told, however, that the laborer, himself, can "jump" the "claim" of the very man who employs him, if he pleases so to do. This is seldom, if ever, done; the person who is willing to be hired, generally prefers to receive the six dollars *per diem*,[4] of which he is

---

[1] bar—sand bar, ridge of sand or gravel in a body of water.

[2] monte-dealers—gamblers.

[3] Pandemonium—In John Milton's *Paradise Lost*, Pandemonium is the palace in hell that Satan and the devils inhabit.

[4] *per diem*—per day.

sure in any case, to running the risk of a "claim" not proving valuable. After all, the "holding of claims" by **proxy**[5] is considered rather as a carrying out of the spirit of the law, than as an evasion of it. But there are many ways of *really* outwitting this rule, though I cannot stop now to relate them, which give rise to innumerable arbitrations, and nearly every Sunday, there is a "miners' meeting" connected with this subject.

Having got our gold mines discovered, and "claimed," I will try to give you a faint idea of how they "work" them. Here, in the mountains, the labor of excavation is extremely difficult, on account of the immense rocks which form a large portion of the soil. Of course, no man can "work out" a "claim" alone. For that reason, and also for the same that makes partnerships desirable, they congregate in companies of four or six, generally designating themselves by the name of the place from whence the majority of the members have emigrated; as for example, the "Illinois," "Bunker Hill," "Bay State," etc., companies. In many places the surface-soil, or in mining-phrase, the "top dirt," "pays" when worked in a "Long Tom." This machine, (I have never been able to discover the derivation of its name,) is a trough, generally about twenty feet in length, and eight inches in depth, formed of wood, with the exception of six feet at one end, called the "riddle," (query, why riddle?[6]) which is made of sheet-iron, perforated with holes about the size of a large marble. Underneath this cullender-like[7] portion of the "long-tom," is placed another trough, about ten feet long, the sides six inches perhaps in height, which divided through the middle by a slender slat, is called the "riffle-box." It takes several persons to manage, properly, a "long-tom." Three or four men station themselves with spades, at the head of the machine,

---

[5] **proxy**—one person acting in place of another.

[6] why riddle?—*riddle* was another name for a sieve.

[7] cullender-like—resembling a colander, or strainer.

while at the foot of it, stands an individual armed "wid de shovel and de hoe." The spadesmen throw in large quantities of the precious dirt, which is washed down to the "riddle" by a stream of water leading into the "long-tom" through wooden gutters or "sluices." When the soil reaches the "riddle," it is kept constantly in motion by the man with the hoe. Of course, by this means, all the dirt and gold escapes through the perforations into the "riffle-box" below, one compartment of which is placed just beyond the "riddle." Most of the dirt washes over the sides of the "riffle-box," but the gold being so astonishingly heavy remains safely at the bottom of it. When the machine gets too full of stones to be worked easily, the man whose business it is to attend to them throws them out with his shovel, looking carefully among them as he does so for any pieces of gold, which may have been too large to pass through the holes of the "riddle." I am sorry to say that he generally loses his labor. At night they "pan out" the gold, which has been collected in the "riffle box" during the day. Many of the miners decline washing the "top dirt" at all, but try to reach as quickly as possible the "bed-rock," where are found the richest deposits of gold. The river is supposed to have formerly flowed over this "bed-rock," in the "**crevices**"[8] of which, it left, as it passed away, the largest portions of the so eagerly sought for ore. The group of mountains amidst which we are living is a spur of the Sierra Nevada; and the "bed-rock," (which in this vicinity is of slate) is said to run through the entire range, lying, in distance varying from a few feet to eighty or ninety, beneath the surface of the soil. . . .

Gold mining is Nature's great lottery scheme. A man may work in a claim for many months, and be poorer at the end of the time than when he commenced; or he may "take out" thousands in a few hours. It is a mere matter

---

[8] **crevices**—cracks.

of chance. A friend of ours, a young Spanish surgeon from Guatemala, a person of intelligence and education, told us that, after "working a claim" for six months, he had taken out but six ounces.

It must be acknowledged, however, that if a person "work his claim" himself, is economical and industrious, keeps his health, and is satisfied with small gains, he is "bound" to make money. And yet, I cannot help remarking, that almost all with whom we are acquainted seem to have *lost*. Some have had their "claims" jumped; many holes which had been excavated, and prepared for working at a great expense, caved in during the heavy rains of the fall and winter. Often after a company has spent an immense deal of time and money in "sinking a shaft," the water from the springs, (the greatest obstacle which the miner has to contend with in this vicinity) rushes in so fast, that it is impossible to work in them, or to contrive any machinery to keep it out, and for that reason only, men have been compelled to abandon places where they were at the very time "taking out" hundreds of dollars a day. If a fortunate or an unfortunate (which shall I call him?) *does* happen to make a "big strike," he is almost sure to fall into the hands of the professed gamblers, who soon relieve him of all care of it. They have not troubled the Bar much during the winter, but as the spring opens, they flock in like **ominous**[9] birds of prey. Last week one left here, after a stay of four days, with over a thousand dollars of the hard-earned gold of the miners. But enough of these best-beloved of Beelzebub,[10] so infinitely worse than the robber or murderer;—for surely it would be kinder to take a man's life, than to poison him with the fatal passion for gambling.

Perhaps you would like to know what class of men is most numerous in the mines. As well as I can judge, there are upon this river as many foreigners as

---

[9] **ominous**—threatening.
[10] Beelzebub—name for the devil.

Americans. The former, with a few exceptions, are extremely ignorant and degraded; though we have the pleasure of being acquainted with three or four Spaniards of the highest education and accomplishments. Of the Americans, the majority are of the better class of mechanics. Next to these, in number, are the sailors and the farmers. There are a few merchants and steamboat-clerks, three or four physicians, and one lawyer. We have no ministers, though fourteen miles from here there is a "Rancho," kept by a man of distinguished appearance, an accomplished monte-dealer and horse-jockey, who is *said* to have been—in the States—a preacher of the Gospel. I know not if this be true; but at any rate, such things are not uncommon in California.

QUESTIONS TO CONSIDER

1. From Clappe's account, what type of individuals were drawn to the gold fields?

2. During the California gold rush, how was a mining claim established?

3. How was a "long-tom" operated?

4. Clappe observed, "Gold mining is Nature's great lottery scheme." What did she mean?

Cattle Drives

BY JOSEPH G. MCCOY

At the end of the Civil War, when cattle were scarce and meat prices high, Joseph G. McCoy (1837–1915) became interested in trying to transport cattle from the ranges of Texas to the markets of Chicago and other big northern cities. In 1867 the first cattle were driven up the Chisholm Trail from Texas to the railroad at Abilene, Kansas, where they were shipped east. The next two decades were the great era of the cowboy and the cattle drive. McCoy provided a complete account of the cattle business in his book Historic Sketches of the Cattle Trade of the West and Southwest *(1874).*

We left the herd fairly started upon the trail for the northern market. Of these trails there are several, one leading to Baxter Springs and Chetopa, another called the "old Shawnee trail" leaving Red River and running eastward, crossing the Arkansas not far above Fort Gibson, thence[1] bending westward up the Arkansas river; but the principal trail now traveled is more direct

---

[1] thence—from there.

and is known as "Chisholm Trail," so named from a semi-civilized Indian who is said to have traveled it first. It is more direct, has more prairie, less timber, more small streams and less large ones, and altogether better grass and fewer flies—no civilized Indian tax[2] or wild Indian disturbances—than any other route yet driven over, and is also much shorter in distance because direct from Red River to Kansas. Twenty-five to thirty-five days is the usual time required to bring a **drove**[3] from Red River to the southern line of Kansas, a distance of between 250 and 300 miles, and an excellent country to drive over. So many cattle have been driven over the trail in the last few years that a broad highway is tread out looking much like a national highway; so plain, a fool could not fail to keep in it.

One remarkable feature is observable as being worthy of note, and that is how completely the herd becomes broken to follow the trail. Certain cattle will take the lead, and others will select certain places in the line, and certain ones bring up the rear, and the same cattle can be seen at their post, marching along like a column of soldiers, every day during the entire journey, unless they become lame, when they will fall back to the rear. A herd of one thousand cattle will stretch out from one to two miles whilst traveling on the trail, and is a very beautiful sight, inspiring the **drover**[4] with enthusiasm **akin**[5] to that enkindled in the breast of the military by the sight of marching columns of men. Certain cowboys are appointed to ride beside the leaders and so control the herd, whilst others ride beside and behind, keeping everything in its place and moving on, the camp wagon and "cavvie-yard"[6] bringing up the rear. When an ordinary

---

[2] civilized Indian tax—charge levied by some tribes to allow cattle drives across their lands.

[3] **drove**—herd.

[4] **drover**—person who drives cattle.

[5] **akin**—like.

[6] "cavvie-yard"—herd of spare horses.

creek or small river is reached the leaders are usually easily **induced**[7] to go in, and although it may be swimming, yet they scarce hesitate, but plunge through to the northern shore and continue the journey, the balance of the herd following as fast as they arrive. Often, however, at large rivers, when swollen by floods, difficulty is experienced in getting over, especially is this the case when the herd gets massed together. Then they become unwieldy and are hard to induce to take to the water. Sometimes days are spent, and much damage to the condition of the herd done, in getting across a single stream. But if the herd is well broken and properly managed, this difficulty is not often experienced.

As soon as the leaders can be induced to take to the water, and strike out for the opposite shore, the balance will follow with but little trouble. Often the drover can induce the leaders to follow him into and across the river, by riding ahead of them into the water and, if need be, swimming his horse in the lead to the opposite shore, whilst the entire herd follow much in the same order that it travels on the trail. It sometimes occurs that the herd will become unmanageable and frightened after entering the water and refuse to strike out to either shore, but gather around their leaders and swim in a circle round and round very similar to milling on the ground when frightened. The aspect is that of a mass of heads and horns, the bodies being out of sight in the water, and it is not uncommon to lose numbers by drowning. When the herd gets to milling in the water—to break this mill and induce the leaders to launch out for the shore the drover swims his cow pony into the center of the mill and, if possible, frightens the mass of struggling whirling cattle, into separation. Not unfrequently the drover is unhorsed and compelled to swim for his life; often taking a swimming steer by the tail, and thus be safely and speedily towed to the shore.

[7] **induced**—persuaded.

Swimming herds of cattle across swollen rivers is not listed as one of the pleasurable events in the drover's trip to the northern market. It is the scarcity of large rivers that constitutes one of the most powerful arguments in favor of the Chisholm trail. Nevertheless it is not entirely free from this objection, especially during rainy seasons. When the herd is over the stream the next job is to get the camp wagon over. This is done by drawing it near the water's edge and, after detaching the oxen and swimming them over, a number of picket ropes are tied together, sufficient to reach across the river, and attached to the wagon which is then pushed into the water and drawn to the opposite shore, whereupon the team is attached and the wagon drawn on to solid ground.

Few occupations are more cheerful, lively and pleasant than that of the cowboy on a fine day or night; but when the storm comes, then is his manhood and often his skill and bravery put to test. When the night is inky dark and the **lurid**[8] lightning flashes its zig-zag course athwart[9] the heavens, and the coarse thunder jars the earth, the winds moan fresh and lively over the prairie, the electric balls[10] dance from tip to tip of the cattle's horns, then the position of the cowboy on duty is **trying**[11] far more than romantic.

When the storm breaks over his head, the least occurrence unusual, such as the breaking of a dry weed or stick, or a sudden and near flash of lightning, will start the herd, as if by magic, all at an instant, upon a wild rush. And woe to the horse, or man, or camp that may be in their path. The only possible show for safety is to mount and ride with them until you can get outside the stampeding column. It is customary to train cattle to

---

[8] **lurid**—unnaturally bright.

[9] athwart—across.

[10] electric balls—natural electrical discharges that look like fire.

[11] **trying**—distress-producing.

listen to the noise of the herder, who sings in a voice more **sonorous**[12] than musical a lullaby consisting of a few short monosyllables. A stranger to the business of stock driving will scarce credit the statement that the wildest herd will not run so long as they can hear distinctly the voice of the herder above the din of the storm. But if by any mishap the herd gets off on a real stampede, it is by bold, dashing, reckless riding in the darkest of nights, and by **adroit**,[13] skillful management that it is checked and brought under control. The moment the herd is off, the cowboy turns his horse at full speed down the retreating column, and seeks to get up beside the leaders, which he does not attempt to stop suddenly, for such an effort would be **futile**,[14] but turns them to the left or right hand, and gradually curves them into a circle, the circumference of which is narrowed down as fast as possible, until the whole herd is rushing wildly round and round on as small a piece of ground as possible for them to occupy. Then the cowboy begins his lullaby note in a loud voice, which has a great effect in quieting the herd. When all is still, and the herd well over its scare, they are returned to their bed-ground, or held where stopped until daylight.

---

[12] **sonorous**—deep and loud.

[13] **adroit**—expert.

[14] **futile**—useless.

QUESTIONS TO CONSIDER

1. What did McCoy see as the advantages of the Chisholm Trail?

2. In normal times, how did cowboys control the cattle?

3. How did cowboys control the cattle in a stampede?

4. McCoy was a cattle dealer. How do you think a working cowboy's view of a cattle drive would have differed from his?

Chinese Workers

The discovery of gold in California in 1848 brought many Chinese immigrants to the United States. When they reached the land they called "Gold Mountain," they usually encountered prejudice, hardship, and violence. Many of these Chinese newcomers worked as laborers on the construction of the transcontinental railroad in the late 1860s. In his book How We Built the Union Pacific Railroad, *Grenville Dodge (1831–1916), chief engineer of the Union Pacific, described troubles between Irish and Chinese railroad workers. An 1875* English-Chinese Phrase Book *suggests the kinds of problems that were encountered by the Chinese in America. In 1882 the Chinese Exclusion Act barred further immigration from China and restricted the rights of earlier Chinese immigrants.*

from *How We Built the Union Pacific Railroad*
by Grenville M. Dodge

Between Ogden and Promontory each company[1] graded a line, running side by side, and in some places one line was right above the other. The laborers upon the Central Pacific were Chinamen, while ours were

---

[1] The transcontinental railroad was built by two companies—the Union Pacific and the Central Pacific.

Irishmen, and there was much ill-feeling between them. Our Irishmen were in the habit of firing their blasts[2] in the cuts[3] without giving the warning to the Chinamen on the Central Pacific working right above them. From this cause several Chinamen were severely hurt. Complaint was made to me by the Central Pacific people, and I **endeavored**[4] to have the contractors bring all hostilities to a close, but, for some reason or other, they failed to do so. One day the Chinamen, appreciating the situation, put in what is called a "grave" on their work, and when the Irishmen right under them were all at work let go their blast and buried several of our men. This brought about a truce at once. From that time the Irish laborers showed due respect for the Chinamen, and there was no further trouble.

from *An English-Chinese Phrase Book*
by Wong Sam and Assistants

你愛點樣價銀	What do you ask for them?
你舷減少些	Can you take less for them?
先生　不舷	I cannot, sir.
汝還有好過汝樣麼	Have you any other kind better than these?
價銀太高	The price is too high.
我唔舷俾得咁多	I am not able to pay.
孩子我都不騙	I don't cheat, even a boy.
先驗明貨正買	Examine your goods before you buy.
因讚稅餉太重	Because the **duty**[5] is too heavy.

---

[2] firing their blasts—setting off dynamite.

[3] cuts—excavated passages in which railroad tracks are laid.

[4] **endeavored**—tried.

[5] **duty**—tax levied on imported goods.

不防我騙汝	Don't fear I am cheating you.
我唔相信汝	I cannot trust you.
信道理捱欺	Christians bear great trials.
佢強搶我物	He took it from me by violence.
我無意打佢	I struck him accidentally.
我認唔該佢還想來打我	I have made an apology, but still he wants to strike me.
佢無事打我	He assaulted me without provocation.
我貸汝樓要汝包水	I will rent the house if you include water.
裝滿箱蘋果	The box contains apples.
女人暈倒在會堂	The lady fainted in church.
佢想白認我行李	He tried to obtain my baggage by false pretenses.
佢強搶我泥口	He claimed my mine.
佢強霸我地	He squatted on my lot.
佢逼勒我可銀	He tries to extort money from me.
逼佢招出	The confession was extorted from him by force.
佢受大頭人定佢罪	He was convicted by a jury.
佢如今定罪	He is now a convict.
佢騙了我之工艮	He cheated me out of my wages.
我日出起身	I arise at sunrise.
煩汝與我付此信	Please send this letter for me.

Chinese Exclusion Act

An act to execute certain treaty **stipulations**[6] relating to Chinese.

WHEREAS, in the opinion of the Government of the United States the coming of Chinese laborers to this country endangers the good order of certain localities within the territory thereof: Therefore,

Be it enacted, That from and after the expiration of ninety days next after the passage of this act, and until the expiration of ten years next after the passage of this act, the coming of Chinese laborers to the United States be, . . . suspended; and during such suspension it shall not be lawful for any Chinese laborer to come, or, having so come after the expiration of said ninety days, to remain within the United States.

SEC. 2. That the master of any vessel who shall knowingly bring within the United States on such vessel, and land or permit to be landed, any Chinese laborer, from any foreign port or place, shall be deemed guilty of a misdemeanor,[7] and on conviction thereof shall be punished by a fine of not more than five hundred dollars for each and every such Chinese laborer so brought, and may be also imprisoned for a term not exceeding one year.

SEC. 3. That the two foregoing sections shall not apply to Chinese laborers who were in the United States on the seventeenth day of November, eighteen hundred and eighty, or who shall have come into the same before the expiration of ninety days next after the passage of this act, . . .

---

[6] **stipulations**—terms or conditions specified in an agreement.

[7] misdemeanor—criminal offense less serious than a felony.

SEC. 6. That in order to the faithful execution of articles one and two of the treaty in this act before mentioned, every Chinese person other than a laborer who may be entitled by said treaty and this act to come within the United States, and who shall be about to come to the United States, shall be identified as so entitled by the Chinese Government in each case, such identity to be evidenced by a certificate issued under the authority of said government, which certificate shall be in the English language or (if not in the English language) accompanied by a translation into English, stating such right to come, and which certificate shall state the name, title, or official rank, if any, the age, height, and all physical peculiarities, former and present occupation or profession and place of residence in China of the person to whom the certificate is issued and that such person is entitled conformably[8] to the treaty in this act mentioned to come within the United States. . . .

SEC. 12. That no Chinese person shall be permitted to enter the United States by land without producing to the proper office of customs the certificate in this act required of Chinese persons seeking to land from a vessel. Any Chinese person found unlawfully within the United States shall be caused to be removed therefrom to the country from whence he came, by direction of the President of the United States, and at the cost of the United States, after being brought before some justice, judge, or commissioner of a court of the United States and found to be one not lawfully entitled to be or remain in the United States.

SEC. 13. That this act shall not apply to diplomatic and other officers of the Chinese Government traveling upon the business of that government, whose credentials

---

[8] conformably—in agreement with the terms (of).

shall be taken as equivalent to the certificate in this act mentioned, and shall exempt them and their body and household servants from the provisions of this act as to other Chinese persons.

SEC. 14. That hereafter no State court or court of the United States shall admit Chinese to citizenship; and all laws in conflict with this act are hereby repealed.

SEC. 15. That the words "Chinese laborers," whenever used in this act, shall be construed to mean both skilled and unskilled laborers and Chinese employed in mining.

QUESTIONS TO CONSIDER

1. According to Dodge's account, why did the Chinese railroad workers resort to violence to stop the Irish from injuring them with their blasting?

2. What kinds of problems does *An English-Chinese Phrase Book* indicate were being experienced by Chinese in the United States in the late 1800s?

3. How did the Chinese Exclusion Act justify barring Chinese laborers from coming to the United States?

Destruction of the Buffalo

BY FRANK H. MAYER

During construction of the transcontinental railroad in the late 1860s, the railroad companies hired buffalo hunters to supply their workers with fresh meat. In the 1870s, the trade in buffalo hides and bones ensured that the slaughter of the herds continued. In a tragically short time, buffalo were nearly exterminated. The traditional way of life of the Indians of the Great Plains, which had been based on the great herds of buffalo that provided them with food, clothing, and shelter, was also destroyed. In his memoir The Buffalo Harvest, *former buffalo hunter Frank H. Mayer described the final phase of the destruction of the buffalo.*

One Sunday morning when I was in camp cutting my own hair, a man rode up on a buckskin gelding.[1] He was typical of his day, tall, slender, grim and determined in visage;[2] he had about him what is called "the look of eagles."

---

[1] buckskin gelding—grayish-yellow male horse that had been neutered.

[2] visage—facial appearance.

I recognized him: he was Charley Jones, from around Garden City. Jones had been a successful runner[3] for several seasons. Then he got disgusted with the slaughter, wrapped his Sharps rifle around one of the wheels of his wagon, and vowed he'd never again set a trigger on a buffer.[4] And he never did.

"Mayer," he began after the usual **amenities**[5] and a stiff drink of corn whiskey, "Mayer, you and the other runners are a passel of . . . fools the way you are wiping out the buffalo. Don't you realize that in just a few years there won't be a . . . buff left in the world?"

I pooh-poohed at this kind of talk.

"Jones, you're clear off on the wrong side of the horse," I told him. "Why, there are as many buffalo now as there ever were. There are hundreds of millions of them."

"Are you getting as many as you used to?"

"Well, no. But that's my fault. I am hunting in the wrong place."

"Where's the right place?" Jones persisted.

"Darned if I know, but we are about to take off and find it tomorrow," I told him.

"You'll never find it," said he. "Because it just don't exist any longer. Unless we're mighty careful there won't even be a specimen to keep in a zoo."

And with that he rode away. I thought, of course, he was loco,[6] and told my boys about it. We did have a deep conference that day, though, and decided that there were, indeed, fewer buffalo than there used to be, but still plenty to keep us going until we were old men whose hands shook so badly they couldn't hold a rifle steady enough to hit one. . . .

But I soon found out how wrong I was.

---

[3] runner—buffalo hunter.

[4] buffer—buffalo.

[5] **amenities**—courtesies.

[6] loco—crazy.

I found it out every day when I went out scouting for something to shoot. A couple of years before it was nothing to see 5,000, 10,000 buff in a day's ride. Now if I saw 50 I was lucky. Presently all I saw was rotting red carcasses or bleaching white bones. We had killed the golden goose. During my runner's years I, quite naturally, wasn't interested in overall figures on total number killed, shipped, and so forth. I was a runner, not a statistician. But if I'd had sense enough in those days I could have realized in a few minutes' time that the game was on the way out. I couldn't have done anything about it, but I could have foreseen that my future was rather dim as a buffalo runner.

Completely accurate figures will likely never be compiled, but here are some authentic ones from the Southwest Historical Society which will show how thoroughly we killed the golden goose.

Dodge City, Kansas, was known as the buffalo city, and more hides were shipped from there than from anywhere else. The shipments started in earnest in 1871, but figures for that year are missing. During the winter of 1872–1873, one firm alone out of Dodge City shipped 200,000 hides. During the same year the same firm handled 1,617,000 pounds of buffalo meat, and $2,500,000 worth of buffalo bones. Now, that was big business in a small frontier town; and remember Dodge, although largest handler of buffalo hides and meat, was only one of a dozen cities that were on rails and shipping buffalo.

But notice how swiftly the traffic dropped. The buffalo years were only seven, 1871 to 1878. The last big shipment was in 1878. It consisted of 40,000 hides, only a fifth of the number handled by the same firm from the same railhead seven years before. After that there weren't enough buffalo left to make handling profitable, so agents shut up their offices and got into some other racket, usually cattle, for fast on the heels of the buffalo came the cattle drives. Again Dodge assumed importance, took on a leading role.

Here are some other figures confirming the Dodge City figure I just cited. In 1872, figures show that 1,491,489 buffalo were killed. In 1873, the high year, the figure given is 1,508,568. Now note this: in 1874, the total is only 158,583—the buffalo was **decimated**[7] in just one year. Tragic picture, don't you think? If you want to add the total killed during those three years you will see it comes to 3,158,730. But the Indian was getting his share, too, and Indian kills are set down by men who study records carefully enough to be listened to and believed, at 405,000 a year, or 1,215,000 in the three-year period. Add the Indian crop to the white runners' crop and you will have a total kill for years 1872, 1873, and 1874 of 4,373,730 animals; in three years' time. No one can say how many were killed during the seven-year period the buffalo harvest lasted, but it must have been well over five million and might even have been close to six. Who knows? . . .

What happens whenever the **law of diminishing returns**[8] sets to work, increased efficiency, happened on the buffalo ranges. I know when I started in we were wasteful. We shot only cows. Their fur was softer; their skins were thinner; they were more in demand. If we killed a bull or two and we killed more than one or two just for the devil of it, we didn't bother to skin him; just left him lay for the wolves and coyotes to come along and do our job for us.

Later on, we were glad to kill bulls, calves, anything.

We were wasteful of hides, too, and I have figures showing how we got over that and increased our efficiency in handling. In 1872, for instance, every hide that reached market represented three or four buffalo killed.

---

[7] **decimated**—greatly reduced.

[8] **law of diminishing returns**—economic principle: after a certain point, increases in investment (or effort) no longer bring increases in returns.

The others were wasted by improper handling, rotting on the ground, and similar shiftlessnesses.[9] The next year we began to tighten up a little: for every hide reaching railhead two buffalo gave their only lives. And in 1874, each hide represented the death of one and a-fourth buffalo. Yes, we became efficient, economical when we had nothing to be efficient or economical about. Our efficiency came too late. We learned our profession, but had no chance to practice it, which is always a tragedy. One by one we runners put up our buffalo rifles, sold them, gave them away, or kept them for other hunting, and left the ranges. And there settled over them a vast quiet, punctuated at night by the snarls and howls of prairie wolves as they prowled through the **carrion**[10] and found living very good. Not a living thing, aside from these wolves and coyotes stirred.

The buffalo was gone.

---

[9] shiftlessnesses—inefficiencies.
[10] **carrion**—remains of dead animals.

QUESTIONS TO CONSIDER

1. What was Mayer's initial response to Charley Jones's claim that the buffalo were being destroyed?

2. What convinced him that Jones was right?

3. What effect did the diminishing herds have on the habits of the buffalo hunters?

Farming on the Great Plains

BY HAMLIN GARLAND

In the late 1800s, hundreds of thousands of farm families settled on the Great Plains. These settlers faced many problems, including lack of water, a harsh climate, and social isolation. Born in western Wisconsin and raised in Iowa, Hamlin Garland (1860–1940) knew firsthand the life on the farming frontier. In his autobiographical work A Son of the Middle Border, *he describes the joys and hardships of farming the Great Plains.*

Spring came to us that year with such sudden beauty, such sweet significance after our long and depressing winter, that it seemed a release from prison, and when at the close of a warm day in March we heard, pulsing down through the golden haze of sunset, the mellow *boom, boom, boom* of the prairie cock our hearts quickened, for this, we were told, was the certain sign of spring.

Day by day the call of this gay herald of spring was taken up by others until at last the whole horizon was ringing with a sunrise symphony of exultant song,

"Boom, boom, boom!" called the roosters; *"cutta, cutta, wha-whoop-squaw, squawk!"* answered the hens as they fluttered and danced on the ridges—and mingled with their jocund[1] hymn we heard at last the slender, wistful piping of the prairie lark.

With the coming of spring my duties as a teamster[2] returned. My father put me in charge of a harrow,[3] and with old Doll and Queen—quiet and faithful span[4]—I drove upon the field which I had plowed the previous October, there to plod to and fro behind my drag,[5] while in the sky above my head and around me on the mellowing soil the life of the season thickened.

Aided by my team I was able to study at close range the prairie roosters as they assembled for their parade. They had regular "stamping grounds" on certain ridges, where the soil was beaten smooth by the pressure of their restless feet. I often passed within a few yards of them.—I can see them now, the cocks leaping and strutting, with trailing wings and down-thrust heads, displaying their **bulbous**,[6] orange-colored neck ornaments while the hens flutter and squawk in silly delight. All the charm and mystery of that prairie world comes back to me, and I ache with an illogical desire to recover it and hold it, and preserve it in some form for my children.—It seems an injustice that they should miss it, and yet it is probable that they are getting an equal joy of life, an equal exaltation from the opening flowers of the single lilac bush in our city back-yard or from an occasional visit to the lake in Central Park.

Dragging is even more wearisome than plowing, in some respects, for you have no handles to assist you and

---

[1] jocund—joyful.

[2] teamster—driver of draft animals.

[3] harrow—device used to prepare soil for planting.

[4] span—pair of draft animals.

[5] drag—heavy wooden or metal frame drawn over the ground to smooth it.

[6] **bulbous**—swollen.

your heels sinking deep into the soft **loam**[7] bring such **unwonted**[8] strain upon the tendons of your legs that you can scarcely limp home to supper, and it seems that you cannot possibly go on another day,—but you do—at least I did.

There was something relentless as the weather in the way my soldier father ruled his sons, and yet he was neither hard-hearted nor unsympathetic. The fact is easily explained. His own boyhood had been task-filled and he saw nothing unnatural in the regular employment of his children. Having had little play-time himself, he considered that we were having a very comfortable boyhood. Furthermore the country was new and labor scarce. Every hand and foot must count under such conditions.

There are certain **ameliorations**[9] to child-labor on a farm. Air and sunshine and food are plentiful. I never lacked for meat or clothing, and mingled with my records of toil are exquisite memories of the joy I took in following the changes in the landscape, in the notes of birds, and in the play of small animals on the sunny soil.

There were no pigeons on the prairie but enormous flocks of ducks came sweeping northward, alighting at sunset to feed in the fields of stubble. They came in countless **myriads**[10] and often when they settled to earth they covered acres of meadow like some prodigious cataract[11] from the sky. When alarmed they rose with a sound like the rumbling of thunder.

At times the lines of their cloud-like flocks were so unending that those in the front rank were lost in the northern sky, while those in the rear were but dim bands beneath the southern sun.—I tried many times to shoot some of them, but never succeeded, so wary were they.

---

[7] **loam**—soil.

[8] **unwonted**—unaccustomed.

[9] **ameliorations**—advantages.

[10] **myriads**—thousands.

[11] prodigious cataract—huge waterfall.

Brant[12] and geese in formal flocks followed and to watch these noble birds pushing their arrowy lines straight into the north always gave me special joy. On fine days they flew high—so high they were but faint lines against the shining clouds.

I learned to imitate their cries, and often caused the leaders to turn, to waver in their course as I uttered my resounding call.

The sand-hill crane came last of all, loitering north in lonely easeful flight. Often of a warm day, I heard his sovereign cry falling from the **azure**[13] dome, so high, so far his form could not be seen, so close to the sun that my eyes could not detect his solitary, majestic circling sweep. He came after the geese. He was the herald of summer. His brazen, **reverberating**[14] call will forever remain associated in my mind with mellow, pulsating earth, springing grass and cloudless glorious May-time skies.

As my team moved to and fro over the field, ground sparrows rose in countless thousands, flinging themselves against the sky like grains of wheat from out a sower's hand, and their chatter fell upon me like the voices of fairy sprites, invisible and **multitudinous**.[15] Long swift narrow flocks of a bird we called "the prairie-pigeon" swooped over the swells on sounding wing, winding so close to the ground, they seemed at times like slender air-borne serpents,—and always the brown lark whistled as if to cheer my lonely task.

Back and forth across the wide field I drove, while the sun crawled slowly up the sky. It was tedious work and I was always hungry by nine, and **famished**[16] at ten. Thereafter the sun appeared to stand still. My chest caved in and my knees trembled with weakness, but when at

---

[12] Brant—type of goose.

[13] **azure**—blue. Garland is referring to the sky.

[14] **reverberating**—echoing.

[15] **multitudinous**—very numerous.

[16] **famished**—starving.

last the white flag fluttering from a chamber window summoned to the mid-day meal, I started with strength miraculously renewed and called, *"Dinner!"* to the hired hand. Unhitching my team, with eager haste I climbed upon old Queen, and rode at ease toward the barn.

Oh, it was good to enter the kitchen, odorous with fresh biscuit and hot coffee! We all ate like dragons, devouring potatoes and salt pork without end, till mother mildly remarked, "Boys, boys! Don't 'founder' yourselves!"[17]

From such a meal I withdrew **torpid**[18] as a gorged snake, but luckily I had half an hour in which to get my courage back,—and besides, there was always the stirring power of father's **clarion**[19] call. His energy appeared super-human to me. I was in awe of him. He kept track of everything, seemed hardly to sleep and never complained of weariness. Long before the nooning was up, (or so it seemed to me) he began to shout: "Time's up boys. Grab a root!"

And so, lame, stiff and sore, with the **sinews**[20] of my legs shortened, so that my knees were bent like an old man's, I hobbled away to the barn and took charge of my team. Once in the field, I felt better. A subtle change, a mellower charm came over the afternoon earth. The ground was warmer, the sky more **genial**,[21] the wind more amiable, and before I had finished my second "round" my joints were moderately **pliable**[22] and my sinews relaxed.

Nevertheless the temptation to sit on the corner of the harrow and dream the moments away was very great, and sometimes as I laid my tired body down on

---

[17] ". . . Don't 'founder' yourselves!"—Don't become ill by overeating.

[18] **torpid**—sluggish.

[19] **clarion**—loud and clear.

[20] **sinews**—tendons.

[21] **genial**—friendly.

[22] **pliable**—flexible.

the tawny, sunlit grass at the edge of the field, and gazed up at the beautiful clouds sailing by, I wished for leisure to explore their purple valleys.—The wind whispered in the tall weeds, and sighed in the hazel bushes. The dried blades touching one another in the passing winds, spoke to me, and the gophers, glad of escape from their dark, underground prisons, chirped a cheery greeting. Such respites were strangely sweet.

So day by day, as I walked my monotonous round upon the ever mellowing soil, the prairie spring unrolled its beauties before me. I saw the last goose pass on to the north, and watched the green grass creeping up the sunny slopes. I answered the splendid challenge of the loitering crane, and studied the ground sparrow building her grassy nest. The prairie hens began to seek seclusion in the swales,[23] and the pocket gopher, busily mining the sod, threw up his purple-brown mounds of cool fresh earth. Larks, blue-birds and king-birds followed the robins, and at last the full tide of May covered the world with luscious green.

[My sister and brother] returned to school but I was too valuable to be spared. The unbroken land of our new farm demanded the plow and no sooner was the planting on our rented place finished than my father began the work of fencing and breaking the sod of the homestead which lay a mile to the south, glowing like a garden under the summer sun. One day late in May my uncle David (who had taken a farm not far away), drove over with four horses hitched to a big breaking plow and together with my father set to work overturning the primeval sward[24] whereon we were to be "lords of the soil."

I confess that as I saw the tender plants and shining flowers bow beneath the remorseless beam,[25] civilization

---

[23] swales—lowlands.

[24] sward—turf.

[25] beam—bar on a plow that holds the coulter, a blade that cuts the earth in advance of the plowshare.

seemed a sad business, and yet there was something epic, something large-gestured and splendid in the "breaking" season. Smooth, glossy, almost unwrinkled the thick ribbon of jet-black sod rose upon the share[26] and rolled away from the mold-board's[27] glistening curve to tuck itself upside down into the furrow behind the horse's heels, and the picture which my uncle made, gave me pleasure in spite of the sad changes he was making.

The land was not all clear prairie and every ounce of David's great strength was required to guide that eighteen-inch plow as it went ripping and snarling through the matted roots of the hazel thickets, and sometimes my father came and sat on the beam in order to hold the coulter to its work, while the giant driver braced himself to the shock and the four horses strained desperately at their traces.[28] These contests had the quality of a wrestling match but the men always won. My own job was to rake and burn the brush which my father mowed with a heavy scythe.[29]—Later we dug post-holes and built fences but each day was spent on the new land.

Around us, on the swells, gray gophers whistled, and the nesting plover quaveringly called. Blackbirds clucked in the furrow and squat badgers watched with jealous eye the plow's inexorable progress toward their dens. The weather was perfect June. Fleecy clouds sailed like snowy **galleons**[30] from west to east, the wind was strong but kind, and we worked in a glow of satisfied ownership.

Many rattlesnakes ("massasaugas" Mr. Button called them), inhabited the moist spots and father and I killed several as we cleared the ground. Prairie wolves lurked

---

[26] share—plowshare, the plow blade that turns over the earth.

[27] mold-board's—belonging to the curved plate on a plow that cuts the earth.

[28] traces—straps that secure a draft animal to what it pulls.

[29] scythe—tool with a long curving blade.

[30] **galleons**—large sailing ships.

in the groves and swales, but as foot by foot and rod by rod, the steady steel rolled the grass and the hazel brush under, all of these wild things died or hurried away, never to return. Some part of this tragedy I was able even then to understand and regret.

At last the wide "quarter section" lay upturned, black to the sun and the garden that had bloomed and fruited for millions of years, waiting for man, lay torn and ravaged. The tender plants, the sweet flowers, the fragrant fruits, the busy insects, all the swarming lives which had been native here for untold centuries were utterly destroyed. It was sad and yet it was not all loss, even to my thinking, for I realized that over this desolation the green wheat would wave and the corn silks shed their pollen. It was not precisely the romantic valley of our song, but it was a rich and promiseful plot and my father seemed entirely content.

QUESTIONS TO CONSIDER

1. Why did Garland's father work his children so hard?

2. What compensations do there seem to have been for the heavy labor on the prairie farm?

3. What change was Garland's family making to the prairie environment?

Westerners at Work

▲

Two women join other prospectors on their way to the Klondike in Alaska in 1898.

This sheet music cover from an 1853 musical shows miners at work.

Several miners pan for gold in Rockville, North Dakota, in 1889.
▼

▲

A cowboy watches cattle during a roundup on a North Dakota ranch in 1905.

▲
Working together, a cowboy and his horse secure a lassoed steer in this
1919 photograph.

A Chinese immigrant works near a tunnel on the Union Pacific Railroad. ▶

Directors of the Union Pacific stand at a marker indicating the 100th meridian, the eastern border of the Great Plains, in 1866.
▼

▲

This photograph shows the Central Pacific construction camp on April 1, 1869, shortly before the completion of the first transcontinental railroad.

A hunter skinning a buffalo, from the title page of *Harper's Weekly*. ▶

Buffalo slaughter on the Kansas Pacific Railroad. ▼

Preserving a Heritage

Letters and Notes on the North American Indians

BY GEORGE CATLIN

Writing in the mid-1800s, the American painter George Catlin (1796–1872) observed that "the noble races of red men who are now spread over these trackless forests and boundless prairies . . . [are] melting away at the approach of civilization." Early in his career, Catlin formed the objective of creating a huge visual record of Indian cultures, to "rescue from oblivion" the appearance and customs of the Native Americans. (See page 53.) He supplemented the hundreds of paintings and drawings he did of the Indians with a series of books in which he recorded observations and experiences gathered during his travels in the American West.

I have for a long time been of the opinion, that the wilderness of our country afforded models equal to those from which the Grecian sculptors transferred to the marble such inimitable grace and beauty;[1] and I am now more confirmed in this opinion, since I have **immersed**[2] myself in the midst of thousands and tens of thousands of these knights of the forest; whose whole lives are lives of chivalry, and whose daily feats, with their naked limbs, might vie with those of the Grecian youths in the beautiful rivalry of the Olympian games.

No man's imagination, with all the aids of description that can be given to it, can ever picture the beauty and wildness of scenes that may be daily witnessed in this romantic country; of hundreds of these graceful youths, without a care to wrinkle, or a fear to disturb the full expression of pleasure and enjoyment that beams upon their faces—their long black hair mingling with their horses' tails, floating in the wind, while they are flying over the carpeted prairie, and dealing death with their spears and arrows, to a band of **infuriated**[3] buffaloes; or their splendid procession in a war-parade, arrayed in all their gorgeous colors and trappings, moving with most exquisite grace and manly beauty, added to that bold defiance which man carries on his front, who acknowledges no superior on earth, and who is **amenable**[4] to no laws except the laws of God and honor. . . .

The distinctive character of all these Western Indians, as well as their traditions relative to their ancient locations, prove beyond a doubt, that they have been for a very long time located on the soil which they now possess; and in most respects, distinct and unlike those nations who formerly inhabited the Atlantic coast, and who (according to the erroneous opinion of a great part of the world), have fled to the West.

---

[1] Among the most typical products of the artists of ancient Greece were sculptures of ideally beautiful young men and women. Catlin is comparing the beauty of the Indians he saw to the ancient Greek statues.

[2] **immersed**—submerged.

[3] **infuriated**—enraged; maddened.

[4] **amenable**—answerable.

It is for these inoffensive and unoffending people, yet unvisited by the vices of civilized society, that I would proclaim to the world, that it is time, for the honor of our country—for the honor of every citizen of the republic—and for the sake of humanity, that our government should raise her strong arm to save the remainder of them from the **pestilence**[5] which is rapidly advancing upon them. We have gotten from them territory enough, and the country which they now inhabit is most of it too barren of timber for the use of civilized man; it affords them, however, the means and luxuries of savage life; and it is to be hoped that our government will not **acquiesce**[6] in the continued wilful destruction of these happy people.

My heart has sometimes almost bled with pity for them, while amongst them, and witnessing their innocent amusements, as I have contemplated the inevitable bane[7] that was rapidly advancing upon them; without that check from the protecting arm of government, and which alone could shield them from destruction.

What degree of happiness these sons of Nature may attain to in the world, in their own way; or in what proportion they may relish the pleasures of life, compared to the sum of happiness belonging to civilized society, has long been a subject of much doubt, and one which I cannot undertake to decide at this time. I would say thus much, however, that if the thirst for knowledge has **entailed**[8] everlasting miseries on mankind from the beginning of the world; if refined and intellectual pains increase in proportion to our intellectual pleasures, I do not see that we gain much advantage over them on that score; and judging from the full-toned enjoyment which beams from their happy faces, I should give it as my

---

[5] **pestilence**—disease; plague; evil.

[6] **acquiesce**—consent without protest; go along silently.

[7] inevitable bane—unavoidable destruction.

[8] **entailed**—involved as a consequence.

opinion, that their lives were much more happy than ours; that is, if the word happiness is properly applied to the enjoyments of those who have not experienced the light of the Christian religion. I have long looked with the eye of a critic, into the **jovial**[9] faces of these sons of the forest, unfurrowed with cares—where the agonizing feeling of poverty had never stamped distress upon the brow. I have watched the bold, **intrepid**[10] step—the proud, yet dignified **deportment**[11] of Nature's man, in fearless freedom, with a soul unalloyed by mercenary lusts,[12] too great to yield to laws or power except from God. As these independent fellows are all joint-tenants of the soil, they are all rich, and none of the steepings[13] of comparative poverty can strangle their just claims to renown. Who (I would ask) can look without admiring, into a society where peace and harmony **prevail**[14]— where virtue is cherished—where rights are protected, and wrongs are **redressed**[15]—with no laws, but the laws of honor, which are the supreme laws of their land. . . .

I have viewed man in the artless and innocent simplicity of nature, in the full enjoyment of the luxuries which God had bestowed upon him. I have seen him happier than kings or princes *can* be; with his pipe and little ones about him. I have seen him shrinking from civilized approach, which came *with all its vices*, like the *dead of night*, upon him: I have seen raised, too, in that *darkness*, *religion's torch*, and seen him gaze and then retreat like the frightened deer, that are blinded by the light; I have seen him shrinking from the soil and haunts of his boyhood, bursting the strongest ties which bound him to the earth, and its pleasures; I have seen him set

---

[9] **jovial**—happy; cheerful.

[10] **intrepid**—fearless.

[11] **deportment**—conduct; behavior.

[12] unalloyed by mercenary lusts—unaffected by desires for money.

[13] steepings—influences.

[14] **prevail**—are widespread.

[15] **redressed**—corrected.

fire to his wigwam, and smooth over the graves of his fathers; I have seen him ('tis the only thing that will bring them) with tears of grief sliding over his cheeks, clap his hand in silence over his mouth, and take the *last look* over his fair hunting grounds, and turn his face in sadness to the setting sun. All this I have seen performed in Nature's silent dignity and grace, which forsook him not in the last extremity of misfortune and despair; and I have seen as often, the approach of the bustling, busy, talking, whistling, hopping, elated and exulting white man, with the first dip of the ploughshare, making sacrilegious trespass on the bones of the valiant dead. I have seen the *skull*, the *pipe*, and the *tomahawk* rise from the ground together, in interrogations which the **sophistry**[16] of the world can never answer. I have seen thus, in all its forms and features, the grand and irresistible march of civilization. I have seen this splendid Juggernaut[17] rolling on, and beheld its sweeping desolation; and held converse with the happy thousands, living, as yet, beyond its influence, who have not been crushed, nor yet have dreamed of its approach.

I have stood amidst these unsophisticated people, and contemplated with feelings of deepest regret, the certain approach of this overwhelming system, which will inevitably march on and prosper, until reluctant tears shall have watered every rod of this fair land; and from the towering cliffs of the Rocky Mountains, the luckless savage will turn back his swollen eye, over the blue and **illimitable**[18] hunting grounds from whence he has fled, and there contemplate, like Caius Marius[19] on the ruins of Carthage, their splendid desolation.

---

[16] **sophistry**—clever but false reasoning.

[17] Juggernaut—Catlin compares the spread of civilization to the huge cart carrying a statue of the Hindu god Krishna, whose worshippers are said to have thrown themselves under the cart's wheels.

[18] **illimitable**—boundless.

[19] Caius Marius (155–86 B.C.)—Roman general; while in Africa, Marius visited the ruins of the city of Carthage, which the Romans had destroyed in 146 B.C. after their victory over the Carthaginians in the Third Punic War.

QUESTIONS TO CONSIDER

1. What qualities did Catlin admire in the appearance and behavior of young American Indians?

2. Why did Catlin feel the Indians were happier than people in "civilized society"?

3. What attitude did Catlin seem to have toward the settlement of the West by American farmers?

from

A Century of Dishonor

BY HELEN HUNT JACKSON

After she moved to Colorado in 1875, writer Helen Hunt Jackson (1830–1885) began to carefully examine the living conditions of the local Native Americans. The result of her investigations was A Century of Dishonor *(1881), in which she recorded a long history of mistreatment of the Indians by the government and white settlers in the West.*

There are within the limits of the United States between two hundred and fifty and three hundred thousand Indians, exclusive of those in Alaska. . . .

Of these, 130,000 are self-supporting on their own reservations, "receiving nothing from the Government except interest on their own moneys, or **annuities**[1]

---

[1] **annuities**—periodic payments.

granted them in consideration of the cession of their lands to the United States."

This fact alone would seem sufficient to dispose forever of the accusation, so persistently brought against the Indian, that he will not work.

Of the remainder, 84,000 are partially supported by the Government—the interest money due them and their annuities, as provided by treaty, being inadequate to their **subsistence**[2] on the reservations where they are confined. In many cases, however, these Indians furnish a large part of their support—the White River Utes, for instance, who are reported by the Indian Bureau as getting sixty-six per cent. of their living by "root-digging, hunting, and fishing;" the Squaxin band, in Washington Territory, as earning seventy-five per cent., and the Chippewas of Lake Superior as earning fifty per cent. in the same way. These facts also would seem to dispose of the accusation that the Indian will not work. . . .

There is not among these three hundred bands of Indians one which has not suffered cruelly at the hands either of the Government or of white settlers. The poorer, the more insignificant, the more helpless the band, the more certain the cruelty and outrage to which they have been subjected. This is especially true of the bands on the Pacific slope. These Indians found themselves of a sudden surrounded by and caught up in the great influx of gold-seeking settlers, as helpless creatures on a shore are caught up in a tidal wave. There was not time for the Government to make treaties; not even time for communities to make laws. The tale of the wrongs, the oppressions, the murders of the Pacific-slope Indians in the last thirty years would be a volume by itself, and is too monstrous to be believed.

It makes little difference, however, where one opens the record of the history of the Indians; every page and

---

[2] **subsistence**—maintaining life.

every year has its dark stain. The story of one tribe is the story of all, varied only by differences of time and place; but neither time nor place makes any difference in the main facts. Colorado is as greedy and unjust in 1880 as was Georgia in 1830, and Ohio in 1795; and the United States Government breaks promises now as **deftly**[3] as then, and with an added ingenuity from long practice.

One of its strongest supports in so doing is the wide-spread sentiment among the people of dislike to the Indian, of impatience with his presence as a "barrier to civilization," and distrust of it as a possible danger. The old tales of the frontier life, with its horrors of Indian warfare, have gradually, by two or three generations' telling, produced in the average mind something like an hereditary instinct of unquestioning and unreasoning **aversion**[4] which it is almost impossible to dislodge or soften.

There are hundreds of pages of **unimpeachable**[5] testimony on the side of the Indian; but it goes for nothing, is set down as sentimentalism or partisanship, tossed aside and forgotten.

President after president has appointed commission after commission to inquire into and report upon Indian affairs, and to make suggestions as to the best methods of managing them. The reports are filled with eloquent statements of wrongs done to the Indians, of **perfidies**[6] on the part of the Government; they counsel, as earnestly as words can, a trial of the simple and unperplexing **expedients**[7] of telling truth, keeping promises, making fair bargains, dealing justly in all ways and all things. These reports are bound up with the Government's Annual Reports, and that is the end of

---

[3] **deftly**—skillfully.

[4] **aversion**—strong dislike.

[5] **unimpeachable**—above suspicion.

[6] **perfidies**—treacheries.

[7] **expedients**—ways of getting what one wants.

them. It would probably be no exaggeration to say that not one American citizen out of ten thousand ever sees them or knows that they exist, and yet any one of them, circulated throughout the country, read by the right-thinking, right-feeling men and women of this land, would be of itself a "campaign document" that would initiate a revolution which would not subside until the Indians' wrongs were, so far as is now left possible, righted.

In 1869 President Grant appointed a commission of nine men . . . to visit the different Indian reservations, and to "examine all matters appertaining to Indian affairs."

In the report of this commission are such paragraphs as the following: "To assert that 'the Indian will not work' is as true as it would be to say that the white man will not work.

"Why should the Indian be expected to plant corn, fence lands, build houses, or do anything but get food from day to day, when experience has taught him that the product of his labor will be seized by the white man tomorrow? The most industrious white man would become a **drone**[8] under similar circumstances. . . .

"The history of the Government connections with the Indians is a shameful record of broken treaties and unfulfilled promises. The history of the border white man's connection with the Indians is a sickening record of murder, outrage, robbery, and wrongs committed by the former, as the rule, and occasional savage outbreaks and unspeakably barbarous deeds of retaliation by the latter, as the exception. . . .

"The testimony of some of the highest military officers of the United States is on record to the effect that, in our Indian wars, almost without exception, the first aggressions have been made by the white man; and the assertion is supported by every civilian of reputation

---

[8] **drone**—idle person.

who has studied the subject. In addition to the class of robbers and outlaws who find **impunity**[9] in their **nefarious**[10] pursuits on the frontiers, there is a large class of professedly reputable men who use every means in their power to bring on Indian wars for the sake of the profit to be realized from the presence of troops and the expenditure of Government funds in their midst. . . ."

To assume that it would be easy, or by any one sudden stroke of legislative policy possible, to undo the mischief and hurt of the long past, set the Indian policy of the country right for the future, and make the Indians at once safe and happy, is the blunder of a hasty and uninformed judgment. The notion which seems to be growing more **prevalent**,[11] that simply to make all Indians at once citizens of the United States would be a sovereign and instantaneous **panacea**[12] for all their ills and all the Government's perplexities, is a very inconsiderate one. To administer complete citizenship of a sudden, all round, to all Indians, **barbarous**[13] and civilized alike, would be as grotesque a blunder as to dose them all round with any one medicine, irrespective of the symptoms and needs of their diseases. It would kill more than it would cure. Nevertheless, it is true, as was well stated by one of the superintendents of Indian Affairs in 1857, that, "so long as they are not citizens of the United States, their rights of property must remain insecure against invasion. The doors of the federal **tribunals**[14] being barred against them while **wards**[15] and dependents, they can only partially exercise the rights of

---

[9] **impunity**—freedom from punishment.

[10] **nefarious**—evil.

[11] **prevalent**—widely accepted.

[12] **panacea**—cure-all.

[13] **barbarous**—primitive in culture; uncivilized.

[14] **tribunals**—courts.

[15] **wards**—persons under the control of legally appointed guardians. The legal status of Indians at the time was like that of children.

free government, or give to those who make, execute, and construe the few laws they are allowed to enact, dignity sufficient to make them respectable. While they continue individually to gather the crumbs that fall from the table of the United States, idleness, **improvidence**,[16] and indebtedness will be the rule, and industry, thrift, and freedom from debt the exception. The utter absence of individual title to particular lands deprives every one among them of the chief incentive to labor and exertion—the very mainspring on which the prosperity of a people depends."

All judicious plans and measures for their safety and salvation must embody provisions for their becoming citizens as fast as they are fit, and must protect them till then in every right and particular in which our laws protect other "persons" who are not citizens.

There is a disposition in a certain class of minds to be impatient with any protestation against wrong which is unaccompanied or unprepared with a quick and exact scheme of remedy. This is illogical. When pioneers in a new country find a tract of poisonous and swampy wilderness to be reclaimed, they do not withhold their hands from fire and axe till they see clearly which way roads should run, where good water will spring, and what crops will best grow on the redeemed land. They first clear the swamp. So with this poisonous and baffling part of the domain of our national affairs—let us first "clear the swamp."

However great perplexity and difficulty there may be in the details of any and every plan possible for doing at this late day anything like justice to the Indian, however hard it may be for good statesmen and good men to agree upon the things that ought to be done, there certainly is, or ought to be, no perplexity whatever, no difficulty whatever, in agreeing upon certain things that ought not

---

[16] **improvidence**—state of being without provisions for the future, like one with no savings.

to be done, and which must cease to be done before the first steps can be taken toward righting the wrongs, curing the ills, and wiping out the disgrace to us of the present condition of our Indians.

Cheating, robbing, breaking promises—these three are clearly things which must cease to be done. One more thing, also, and that is the refusal of the protection of the law to the Indian's rights of property, "of life, liberty, and the pursuit of happiness."

When these four things have ceased to be done, time, statesmanship, philanthropy, and Christianity can slowly and surely do the rest. Till these four things have ceased to be done, statesmanship and philanthropy alike must work in vain, and even Christianity can reap but small harvest.

QUESTIONS TO CONSIDER

1. How did Jackson argue against the belief that American Indians were unwilling to work?

2. What did Jackson feel would be the chief benefit to the Indians of making them citizens of the United States?

3. What immediate changes did Jackson feel had to be made in the way the Indians were treated?

The Conservation of Natural Resources

BY THEODORE ROOSEVELT

Before Theodore Roosevelt's presidency (1901–1909), the U.S.
government had paid very little attention to America's natural
resources. Public land, forests, mineral deposits, and water—mostly
in the West—had been distributed with little concern for how
they were used or in what condition they were left. In June 1902,
with Roosevelt's backing, Congress passed the National Reclamation
Act, which set aside the bulk of the money secured from the sale of
public lands in the West to pay for the construction of dams. These
dams would provide water to irrigate and restore barren lands, and
the profits from selling this water would fund other conservation
projects. On December 3, 1907, as part of his seventh annual mes-
sage to Congress, Roosevelt reported on this program.

The conservation of our natural resources and their
proper use constitute the fundamental problem which
underlies almost every other problem of our national
life. . . . As a nation we not only enjoy a wonderful
measure of present prosperity but if this prosperity is

used aright[1] it is an **earnest**[2] of future success such as no other nation will have. The reward of foresight for this nation is great and easily foretold. But there must be the look ahead, there must be a realization of the fact that to waste, to destroy, our natural resources, to skin and exhaust the land instead of using it so as to increase its usefulness, will result in undermining in the days of our children the very prosperity which we ought by right to hand down to them amplified and developed. For the last few years, through several agencies, the government has been endeavoring to get our people to look ahead and to substitute a planned and orderly development of our resources in place of a haphazard striving for immediate profit. . . .

The work of the Reclamation Service in developing the larger opportunities of the Western half of our country for irrigation is more important than almost any other movement. The constant purpose of the government in connection with the Reclamation Service has been to use the water resources of the public lands for the ultimate greatest good of the greatest number; in other words, to put upon the land permanent homemakers, to use and develop it for themselves and for their children and children's children. . . .

The effort of the government to deal with the public land has been based upon the same principle as that of the Reclamation Service. The land law system[3] which was designed to meet the needs of the fertile and well-watered regions of the Middle West has largely broken down when applied to the drier regions of the Great Plains, the mountains, and much of the Pacific slope, where a farm of 160 acres is inadequate for self-support. . . . Three years ago a public-lands commission was appointed to

---

[1] aright—correctly.

[2] **earnest**—promise.

[3] land law system—government policies for the distribution of public land, beginning with the Homestead Act of 1862, which granted 160 acres for a nominal fee to anyone who would settle on that land for five years.

scrutinize[4] the law, and defects, and recommend a remedy. Their examination specifically showed the existence of great fraud upon the public domain,[5] and their recommendations for changes in the law were made with the design of conserving the natural resources of every part of the public lands by putting it to its best use. Especial attention was called to the prevention of settlement by the passage of great areas of public land into the hands of a few men, and to the enormous waste caused by unrestricted grazing upon the open range. The recommendations of the Public-Lands Commission are sound, for they are especially in the interest of the actual homemaker; and where the small homemaker cannot at present utilize the land [the recommendations] provide that the government shall keep control of it so that it may not be monopolized by a few men. The Congress has not yet acted upon these recommendations, but they are so just and proper, so essential to our national welfare, that I feel confident, if the Congress will take time to consider them, that they will ultimately be adopted.

Some such legislation as that proposed is essential in order to preserve the great stretches of public grazing-land which are unfit for cultivation under present methods and are valuable only for the **forage**[6] which they supply. These stretches amount in all to some 300,000,000 acres, and are open to the free grazing of cattle, sheep, horses, and goats, without restriction. Such a system, or lack of system, means that the range is not so much used as wasted by abuse. As the West settles, the range becomes more and more overgrazed. Much of it cannot be used to advantage unless it is fenced, for fencing is the only way by which to keep in check the owners of nomad flocks which roam hither and thither,

---

[4] **scrutinize**—study closely; examine carefully.

[5] public domain—public land, that is, land owned by the government.

[6] **forage**—animal food.

utterly destroying the pastures and leaving a waste behind so that their presence is **incompatible**[7] with the presence of homemakers. The existing fences are all illegal. . . . All these fences, those that are hurtful and those that are beneficial, are alike illegal and must come down. But it is an outrage that the law should necessitate such action on the part of the Administration. The unlawful fencing of public lands for private grazing must be stopped, but the necessity which occasioned it must be provided for. The Federal Government should have control of the range, whether by permit or lease, as local necessities may determine. Such control could secure the great benefit of legitimate fencing, while at the same time securing and promoting the settlement of the country. . . . The government should part with its title only to the actual homemaker, not to the profit-maker who does not care to make a home. Our prime object is to secure the rights and guard the interests of the small ranchman, the man who ploughs and pitches hay for himself. It is this small ranchman, this actual settler and homemaker, who in the long run is most hurt by permitting thefts of the public land in whatever form.

Optimism is a good characteristic, but if carried to an excess it becomes foolishness. We are **prone**[8] to speak of the resources of this country as inexhaustible; this is not so. The mineral wealth of the country, the coal, iron, oil, gas, and the like, does not reproduce itself, and therefore is certain to be exhausted ultimately; and wastefulness in dealing with it today means that our descendants will feel the exhaustion a generation or two before they otherwise would. But there are certain other forms of waste which could be entirely stopped—the waste of soil by washing,[9] for instance, which is among the most dangerous of all wastes now in progress in the United States,

---

[7] **incompatible**—not able to exist together.

[8] **prone**—inclined.

[9] washing—erosion.

is easily preventible, so that this present enormous loss of fertility is entirely unnecessary. The preservation or replacement of the forests is one of the most important means of preventing this loss. We have made a beginning in forest preservation, but . . . so rapid has been the rate of exhaustion of timber in the United States in the past, and so rapidly is the remainder being exhausted, that the country is unquestionably on the verge of a timber famine which will be felt in every household in the land. . . . The present annual consumption of lumber is certainly three times as great as the annual growth; and if the consumption and growth continue unchanged, practically all our lumber will be exhausted in another generation, while long before the limit to complete exhaustion is reached the growing scarcity will make itself felt in many blighting ways upon our national welfare. About twenty per cent of our forested territory is now reserved in national forests, but these do not include the most valuable timberlands, and in any event the proportion is too small to expect that the reserves can accomplish more than a **mitigation**[10] of the trouble which is ahead for the nation.

---

[10] **mitigation**—lessening in severity.

QUESTIONS TO CONSIDER

1. In Roosevelt's view, why was conservation of natural resources "the fundamental problem which underlies almost every other problem of our national life"?

2. What did Roosevelt identify as the main purpose of the Reclamation Service?

3. Why was the government land law system unworkable in the West?

4. What did Roosevelt see as the most dangerous of all wastes of natural resources?

The Indian View of Nature

BY LUTHER STANDING BEAR

The American Indians' attitude toward the natural world contrasted sharply with that of the frontier settlers, for whom it was a personal possession to be exploited. To begin with, the idea that land could be divided up and sold to individuals made no sense to the Indians, for whom the earth was a divine gift to be held in common by the people who lived on it. The belief that the earth was divine also affected how the Indians used the land and its animal inhabitants. Lakota Sioux leader Luther Standing Bear (1868–1947?) felt that the Indians "sought the harmony of man with his surroundings, [but whites] sought the dominance of surroundings." In Land of the Spotted Eagle *(1933), one in a series of books he wrote on Indian life, Standing Bear explored the Indian view of nature.*

The Lakota was a true naturist—a lover of Nature. He loved the earth and all things of the earth, the attachment growing with age. The old people came literally to love the soil and they sat or reclined on the ground with a feeling of being close to a mothering power. It was good for the skin to touch the earth and the old people liked to remove their moccasins and walk with bare feet on the sacred earth. Their tipis were built upon the earth and their altars were made of earth. The birds that flew in the air came to rest upon the earth and it was the final abiding place of all things that lived and grew. The soil was soothing, strengthening, cleansing, and healing.

This is why the old Indian still sits upon the earth instead of propping himself up and away from its life-giving forces. For him, to sit or lie upon the ground is to be able to think more deeply and to feel more keenly; he can see more clearly into the mysteries of life and come closer in kinship to other lives about him.

The earth was full of sounds which the old-time Indian could hear, sometimes putting his ear to it so as to hear more clearly. The forefathers of the Lakotas had done this for long ages until there had come to them real understanding of earth ways. It was almost as if the man were still a part of the earth as he was in the beginning, according to the legend of the tribe. This beautiful story of the **genesis**[1] of the Lakota people furnished the foundation for the love they bore for earth and all things of the earth. Wherever the Lakota went, he was with Mother Earth. No matter where he roamed by day or slept by night, he was safe with her. This thought comforted and sustained the Lakota and he was eternally filled with gratitude.

From Wakan Tanka[2] there came a great unifying life force that flowed in and through all things—the flowers of the plains, blowing winds, rocks, trees, birds, animals—and was the same force that had been breathed into the first man. Thus all things were kindred and brought together by the same Great Mystery.

---

[1] **genesis**—origin; coming into being.

[2] Wakan Tanka—"Big Holy," Lakota name for God.

Kinship with all creatures of the earth, sky, and water was a real and active principle. For the animal and bird world there existed a brotherly feeling that kept the Lakota safe among them. And so close did some of the Lakotas come to their feathered and furred friends that in true brotherhood they spoke a common tongue.

The animal had rights—the right of man's protection, the right to live, the right to multiply, the right to freedom, and the right to man's indebtedness—and in recognition of these rights the Lakota never enslaved the animal, and spared all life that was not needed for food and clothing.

This concept of life and its relations was humanizing and gave to the Lakota an abiding love. It filled his being with the joy and mystery of living; it gave him reverence for all life; it made a place for all things in the scheme of existence with equal importance to all. The Lakota could despise no creature, for all were of one blood, made by the same hand, and filled with the essence of the Great Mystery. In spirit the Lakota was humble and meek. "Blessed are the meek: for they shall inherit the earth," was true for the Lakota, and from the earth he inherited secrets long since forgotten. His religion was sane, normal, and human.

Reflection upon life and its meaning, consideration of its wonders, and observation of the world of creatures, began with childhood. The earth, which was called *Maka*, and the sun, called *Anpetuwi*, represented two functions somewhat **analogous**[3] to those of male and female. The earth brought forth life, but the warming, enticing rays of the sun coaxed it into being. The earth yielded, the sun **engendered**.[4]

In talking to children, the old Lakota would place a hand on the ground and explain: "We sit in the lap of our

---

[3] **analogous**—similar.
[4] **engendered**—gave rise to (life).

Mother. From her we, and all other living things, come. We shall soon pass, but the place where we now rest will last forever." So we, too, learned to sit or lie on the ground and become conscious of life about us in its multitude of forms. Sometimes we boys would sit motionless and watch the swallow, the tiny ants, or perhaps some small animal at its work and ponder on its industry and **ingenuity**;[5] or we lay on our backs and looked long at the sky and when the stars came out made shapes from the various groups. The morning and evening star always attracted attention, and the Milky Way was a path which was traveled by the ghosts. The old people told us to heed *wa maka skan*, which were the "moving things of earth." This meant, of course, the animals that lived and moved about, and the stories they told of *wa maka skan* increased our interest and delight. The wolf, duck, eagle, hawk, spider, bear, and other creatures, had marvelous powers, and each one was useful and helpful to us. Then there were the warriors who lived in the sky and dashed about on their spirited horses during a thunder storm, their lances clashing with the thunder and glittering with the lightning. There was *wiwila*, the living spirit of the spring, and the stones that flew like a bird and talked like a man. Everything was possessed of personality, only differing with us in form. Knowledge was **inherent**[6] in all things. The world was a library and its books were the stones, leaves, grass, brooks, and the birds and animals that shared, alike with us, the storms and blessings of earth. We learned to do what only the student of nature ever learns, and that was to feel beauty. We never **railed**[7] at the storms, the furious winds, and the biting frosts and snows. To do so intensified human **futility**,[8] so whatever came we adjusted

---

[5] **ingenuity**—inventiveness.

[6] **inherent**—existing as a permanent, essential quality.

[7] **railed**—complained bitterly.

[8] **futility**—pointlessness.

ourselves, by more effort and energy if necessary, but without complaint. Even the lightning did us no harm, for whenever it came too close, mothers and grandmothers in every tipi put cedar leaves on the coals and their magic kept danger away. Bright days and dark days were both expressions of the Great Mystery, and the Indian reveled in being close to the Big Holy. His worship was **unalloyed**,[9] free from the fears of civilization.

I have come to know that the white mind does not feel toward nature as does the Indian mind, and it is because, I believe, of the difference in childhood instruction. I have often noticed white boys gathered in a city by-street or alley jostling and pushing one another in a foolish manner. They spend much time in this aimless fashion, their natural faculties neither seeing, hearing, nor feeling the varied life that surrounds them. There is about them no awareness, no acuteness, and it is this dullness that gives ugly mannerisms full play; it takes from them natural poise and stimulation. In contrast, Indian boys, who are naturally reared, are alert to their surroundings; their senses are not narrowed to observing only one another, and they cannot spend hours seeing nothing, hearing nothing, and thinking nothing in particular. Observation was certain in its rewards; interest, wonder, admiration grew, and the fact was appreciated that life was more than mere human **manifestation**;[10] that it was expressed in a multitude of forms. This appreciation enriched Lakota existence. Life was vivid and pulsing; nothing was casual and commonplace. The Indian lived—lived in every sense of the word—from his first to his last breath.

The character of the Indian's emotion left little room in his heart for antagonism toward his fellow creatures, this attitude giving him what is sometimes referred to as

---

[9] **unalloyed**—pure; unmixed.

[10] **manifestation**—indication; evidence. Standing Bear means that life is greater than the evidence of humanity alone.

"the Indian point of view." Every true student, every lover of nature has "the Indian point of view," but there are few such students, for few white men approach nature in the Indian manner. The Indian and the white man sense things differently because the white man has put distance between himself and nature; and assuming a lofty place in the scheme of order of things has lost for him both reverence and understanding. Consequently the white man finds Indian philosophy **obscure**[11]— wrapped, as he says, in a maze of ideas and symbols which he does not understand. A writer friend, a white man whose knowledge of "Injuns" is far more **profound**[12] and sympathetic than the average, once said that he had been privileged, on two occasions, to see the contents of an Indian medicine-man's bag in which were bits of earth, feathers, stones, and various other articles of symbolic nature; that a "collector" showed him one and laughed, but a great and world-famous archeologist showed him the other with admiration and wonder. Many times the Indian is embarrassed and baffled by the white man's **allusions**[13] to nature in such terms as crude, primitive, wild, rude, untamed, and savage. For the Lakota, mountains, lakes, rivers, springs, valleys, and woods were all finished beauty; winds, rain, snow, sunshine, day, night, and change of seasons brought interest; birds, insects, and animals filled the world with knowledge that defied the **discernment**[14] of man.

But nothing the Great Mystery placed in the land of the Indian pleased the white man, and nothing escaped his transforming hand. Wherever forests have not been mowed down; wherever the animal is recessed in their quiet protection; wherever the earth is not **bereft**[15] of

---

[11] **obscure**—dark and hidden; difficult to understand.

[12] **profound**—deep.

[13] **allusions**—references.

[14] **discernment**—perception; comprehension.

[15] **bereft**—deprived.

four-footed life—that to him is an "unbroken wilderness." But since for the Lakota there was no wilderness; since nature was not dangerous but hospitable; not forbidding but friendly, Lakota philosophy was healthy—free from fear and **dogmatism**.[16] And here I find the great distinction between the faith of the Indian and the white man. Indian faith sought the harmony of man with his surroundings; the other sought the dominance of surroundings. In sharing, in loving all and everything, one people naturally found a measure of the thing they sought; while, in fearing, the other found need of conquest. For one man the world was full of beauty; for the other it was a place of sin and ugliness to be endured until he went to another world, there to become a creature of wings, half-man and half-bird. Forever one man directed his Mystery to change the world He had made; forever this man pleaded with Him to chastise His wicked ones; and forever he implored his Wakan Tanka to send His light to earth. Small wonder this man could not understand the other.

But the old Lakota was wise. He knew that man's heart, away from nature, becomes hard; he knew that lack of respect for growing, living things soon led to lack of respect for humans too. So he kept his youth close to its softening influence.

---

[16] **dogmatism**—narrow, inflexible system of beliefs.

QUESTIONS TO CONSIDER

1. According to Standing Bear, what basic attitude did the Lakota have toward the land itself?

2. What relationship did the Lakota feel they had with the animals with which they shared the land?

3. Standing Bear observed of the Lakota view of nature, "Knowledge was inherent in all things." What did he mean?

4. What link did Standing Bear see between the education of the young and the differing attitudes toward nature of Indians and whites?

5. Why would the Indian attitude toward nature provide a better understanding of ecology?

A Vanishing World

▲ Edward S. Curtis (1868–1952) began photographing Native Americans around 1895. Nine years later, he decided to document the traditional cultures of the Indians of the West. Here he shows a chief of the Klamath people of California and Oregon.

◄ A woman of the Nakoaktok people of the Pacific Northwest practices her art in this Curtis photograph.

▲
The U.S. government introduced Native-American children to white culture by enforcing military-style discipline in schools such as this Indian school in Oklahoma.

Indian children at the school on the Swinomish Reservation in Washington in 1907 give up traditional dress and learn the ways of the dominant culture. ▶

▲

Theodore Roosevelt, who later became an ardent conservationist, worked as a cowboy in North Dakota in 1885.

▲

The early days of automobile tourism in the West are pictured in this 1906 photograph of a resort hotel in the Sierra Nevada Mountains of California.

In 1902 these tourists were photographed in Yosemite Valley, which John Muir had helped establish as a national park in 1890.

In 1901 oil was discovered in Texas at Spindletop Hill, near Beaumont, marking the beginning of the Texas oil industry.

The traditional and the modern West meet in this photograph of Dallas.
▼

186   **The American West**

Interpreting the Past

The Significance of the Frontier in American History

BY FREDERICK JACKSON TURNER

In 1890 the U.S. Census Bureau noted that "frontier" areas, defined as those with fewer than two inhabitants per square mile, no longer formed a continuous line marking a division between wilderness and settlement. At a meeting of the American Historical Association in 1893, historian Frederick Jackson Turner (1861–1932) delivered a paper that changed the direction of the study of American history. Turner identified the official "closing of the frontier" as marking the end of a process of settling the wilderness that he believed had fundamentally shaped American political institutions, society, and character.

In a recent bulletin of the superintendent of the census for 1890 appear these significant words: "Up to and including 1880 the country had a frontier of settlement, but at present the unsettled area has been so broken into by isolated bodies of settlement that there can hardly be said to be a frontier line. In the discussion of its extent, its westward movement, etc., it cannot, therefore, any longer have a place in the census reports." This brief official statement marks the closing of a great historic movement. Up to our own day American history has been in a large degree the history of the colonization of the Great West. The existence of an area of free land, its continuous recession,[1] and the advance of American settlement westward explain American development.

Behind institutions, behind constitutional forms and modifications, lie the vital forces that call these organs[2] into life and shape them to meet changing conditions. The peculiarity of American institutions is the fact that they have been compelled to adapt themselves to the changes of an expanding people—to the changes involved in crossing a continent, in winning a wilderness, and in developing at each area of this progress, out of the primitive economic and political conditions of the frontier, the complexity of city life. Said Calhoun[3] in 1817, "We are great, and rapidly—I was about to say fearfully—growing!" So saying, he touched the distinguishing feature of American life. All peoples show development: the germ theory of politics[4] has been sufficiently emphasized. In the case of most nations, however, the development has occurred in a limited area; and if the nation has expanded, it has met other growing peoples whom it has conquered. But in the case of the United States we have a different **phenomenon**.[5] Limiting our attention to the Atlantic coast, we have the familiar phenomenon of the evolution of institutions in

---

[1] recession—withdrawal.

[2] organs—instruments through which actions are done.

[3] Calhoun—John C. Calhoun (1782–1850), U.S. politician from South Carolina who favored the annexation of Florida and Texas.

[4] germ theory of politics—historical theory that American political institutions derived from ancient Germanic tribal customs.

[5] **phenomenon**—occurrence.

a limited area, such as the rise of representative government; the differentiation of simple colonial governments into complex organs; the progress from primitive industrial society, without **division of labor,**[6] up to manufacturing civilization. But we have in addition to this *a recurrence of the process of evolution in each Western area reached in the process of expansion.* Thus American development has exhibited not merely advance along a single line but a return to primitive conditions on a continually advancing frontier line, and a new development for that area. American social development has been continually beginning over again on the frontier. This perennial rebirth, this fluidity of American life, this expansion westward with its new opportunities, its continuous touch with the simplicity of primitive society, furnish the forces dominating American character. The true point of view in the history of this nation is not the Atlantic coast, it is the Great West. Even the slavery struggle occupies its important place in American history because of its relation to westward expansion.

In this advance the frontier is the outer edge of the wave—the meeting point between savagery and civilization. Much has been written about the frontier from the point of view of border warfare and the chase, but as a field for the serious study of the economist and the historian it has been neglected.

What is the [American] frontier? It is not the European frontier—a fortified boundary line running through dense populations. The most significant thing about it is that it lies at the **hither**[7] edge of free land. In the census reports it is treated as the margin of that settlement which has a density of two or more to the square mile. The term is an elastic one, and for our purpose does not need sharp definition. We shall consider the

---

[6] **division of labor**—separation of production processes into tasks assigned to different workers.

[7] **hither**—near.

whole frontier belt, including the Indian country and the outer margin of the "settled area" of the census reports. This paper will make no attempt to treat the subject exhaustively; its aim is simply to call attention to the frontier as a fertile field for investigation, and to suggest some of the problems which arise in connection with it.

In the settlement of America we have to observe how European life entered the continent, and how America modified and developed that life, and reacted on Europe. . . . The frontier is the line of most rapid and effective Americanization. The wilderness masters the colonist. It finds him a European in dress, industries, tools, modes of travel, and thought. It takes him from the railroad car and puts him in the birch canoe. It strips off the garments of civilization, and arrays him in the hunting shirt and the moccasin. It puts him in the log cabin of the Cherokee and the Iroquois, and runs an Indian **palisade**[8] around him. Before long he has gone to planting Indian corn and plowing with a sharp stick; he shouts the war cry and takes the scalp in orthodox Indian fashion. In short, at the frontier the environment is at first too strong for the man. He must accept the conditions which it furnishes, or perish, and so he fits himself into the Indian clearings and follows the Indian trails. Little by little he transforms the wilderness. . . . The fact is that here is a new product that is American. At first the frontier was the Atlantic coast. It was the frontier of Europe in a very real sense. Moving westward, the frontier became more and more American. *As successive terminal moraines result from successive glaciations,*[9] *so each frontier leaves its traces behind it, and when it becomes a settled area the region still partakes of the frontier characteristics.* Thus the advance of the frontier has meant a steady movement away from the influence of Europe, a steady growth of independence

---

[8] **palisade**—fence.

[9] *terminal moraines . . . glaciations*—terminal moraines are the debris left behind by a retreating glacier.

on American lines. And to study this advance, the men who grew up under these conditions, and the political, economic, and social results of it, is to study the really American part of our history.

Intellectual Traits

From the conditions of frontier life came intellectual traits of profound importance. The works of travelers along each frontier from colonial days onward describe for each certain traits, and these traits have, while softening down, still persisted as survivals in the place of their origin, even when a higher social organization succeeded. The result is that to the frontier the American intellect owes its striking characteristics. That coarseness and strength combined with **acuteness**[10] and inquisitiveness, that practical, inventive turn of mind, quick to find **expedients**,[11] that masterful grasp of material things, lacking in the artistic but powerful to effect great ends, that restless, nervous energy, that dominant individualism, working for good and for evil, and withal[12] that buoyancy and **exuberance**[13] which comes with freedom, these are traits of the frontier, or traits called out elsewhere because of the existence of the frontier. Since the days when the fleet of Columbus sailed into the waters of the New World, America has been another name for opportunity, and the people of the United States have taken their tone from the **incessant**[14] expansion which has not only been open but has even been forced upon them. He would be a rash prophet who should assert that the expansive character of American life has now entirely ceased. Movement has been its dominant fact, and, unless this training has no effect upon a people, the

---

[10] **acuteness**—sharpness.
[11] **expedients**—suitable solutions.
[12] withal—with it all.
[13] **exuberance**—enthusiasm.
[14] **incessant**—unceasing.

American intellect will continually demand a wider field for its exercise. But never again will such gifts of free land offer themselves. For a moment at the frontier the bonds of custom are broken, and unrestraint is triumphant. There is not *tabula rasa*.[15] The stubborn American environment is there with its **imperious**[16] summons to accept its conditions; the inherited ways of doing things are also there; and yet, in spite of environment, and in spite of custom, each frontier did indeed furnish a new field of opportunity, a gate of escape from the bondage of the past; and freshness, and confidence, and scorn of older society, impatience of its restraints and its ideas, and indifference to its lessons, have accompanied the frontier. What the Mediterranean Sea was to the Greeks, breaking the bond of custom, offering new experiences, calling out new institutions and activities, that, and more, the ever retreating frontier has been to the United States directly, and to the nations of Europe more remotely. And now, four centuries from the discovery of America, at the end of a hundred years of life under the Constitution, the frontier has gone, and with its going has closed the first period of American history.

---

[15] *tabula rasa*—Latin phrase meaning "blank slate."

[16] **imperious**—urgent.

QUESTIONS TO CONSIDER

1. In Turner's view, what process shaped American institutions until the 1890s?

2. How did the American frontier differ from frontier regions in Europe?

3. Turner observed, "The frontier is the line of most rapid and effective Americanization." What did he mean?

4. What American intellectual traits did Turner believe had resulted from the experience of the frontier?

from

The Great Plains

BY WALTER PRESCOTT WEBB

The Great Plains is a region of semiarid flatlands extending from roughly the 100th meridian of longitude (running from eastern Oklahoma to the central Dakotas) westward to the Rocky Mountains. Building on Frederick Jackson Turner's frontier theory, historian Walter Prescott Webb (1888–1963) detailed in his book The Great Plains *what he believed were the specific effects of the landscape and climate of this region on American history and character.*

Why was the West considered Lawless? Was it Really Lawless or did it merely Appear Lawless?

These questions involve us in all sorts of difficulties and elude definite answers. There is, however, some basis for discussion. The most partisan Westerner will admit that the West was considered lawless; the casual visitor from the East was quite certain that it appeared to be lawless; for the sake of this discussion it may be said that the West was lawless and that the Westerner was a persistent lawbreaker. It is to be hoped, however, that the Westerner will withhold his fire until an explanation can be made.

The West was lawless for two reasons: first, because of the social conditions that **obtained**[1] there during the period under consideration; secondly, because the law that was applied there was not made for the conditions that existed and was unsuitable for those conditions. It did not fit the needs of the country, and could not be obeyed.

The social conditions in the Great Plains have already been discussed. We know, for example, that in the early period the restraints of law could not make themselves felt in the **rarefied**[2] population. Each man had to make his own law because there was no other to make it. He had to defend himself and protect his rights by his force of personality, courage, and skill at arms. All men went armed and moved over vast areas among other armed men. The six-shooter was the final **arbiter**,[3] a court of last resort, and an executioner. How could a man live in such a *milieu*[4] and abide by the laws that obtained in the thickly settled portions of the country, where the police gave protection and the courts justice? Could the plainsman go unarmed in a country where danger was ever present? Could a man refuse to use those arms where his own life was at stake? Such men might live in the West, but they could never be of much force. They could not be cowboys or Indian fighters or peace officers or outstanding good citizens.

In the absence of law and in the social conditions that obtained, men worked out an extra-legal code or custom by which they guided their actions. This custom is often called the code of the West. The code demanded what Roosevelt[5] called a square deal; it demanded fair play. According to it one must not shoot his **adversary**[6]

---

[1] **obtained**—existed.

[2] **rarefied**—dispersed; spread out.

[3] **arbiter**—judge.

[4] *milieu*—environment.

[5] Roosevelt—Theodore Roosevelt (1858–1919), U.S. president (1901–1909) whose 1904 political platform was known as "the Square Deal."

[6] **adversary**—enemy; opponent.

in the back, and he must not shoot an unarmed man. In actual practice he must give notice of his intention, albeit[7] the action followed the notice as a lightning stroke. Failure to abide by the code did not necessarily bring formal punishment for the act already committed; it meant that the violator might be cut off without benefit of notice[8] in the next act. Thus was justice carried out in a crude but effective manner, and warning given that in general the code must prevail.

Under the social conditions the taking of human life did not entail the stigma[9] that in more thickly settled regions is associated with it. Men were all equal. Each was his own defender. His survival imposed upon him certain obligations which, if he were a man, he would accept. If he acted according to the code he not only attested his courage but implied that he was skilled in the art of living. Murder was too harsh a word to apply to his performance, a mere incident, as it were. But how could the Easterner, surrounded and protected by the conventions, understand such distinctions?

Theft was another form of lawlessness common on the Great Plains. But the code of the West had its way of interpreting and punishing theft. Of petty thievery there was practically none on the Plains. Property consisted of horses and cattle. There were horse thieves and cattle thieves.

There was no greater crime than to steal a man's horse, to set him afoot. It was like stealing the sailor's ship or the wings of the bird. There were no **extenuating circumstances**[10] and little time for explanation or prayer. The penalty was death. The cow thief was not nearly so bad in public estimation. A cow was mere property, but a horse was life itself to the plainsman. The code of the West made a strange distinction, one that the East has not

---

[7] albeit—although; even if.

[8] notice—warning.

[9] entail the stigma—involve the shame.

[10] **extenuating circumstances**—facts that reduce the seriousness of an event.

understood, between a cow and a **maverick**.[11] A cow that bore a brand was the private property of the man whose brand it bore; a maverick was public property and belonged to the man that branded it, just as the buffalo hide belonged to the one that killed the buffalo. The fact that the maverick was the calf of the branded cow did not affect the situation very much, especially in the early days. There were few cattlemen who did not brand mavericks; but no cattleman considered himself a thief for having done so.

The lawlessness thus far discussed grew out of the social situation in the early days. Other forms of lawlessness arose because the law was wholly inapplicable and unsuited to the West. Some examples will be noticed here.

The land laws were persistently broken in the West because they were not made for the West and were wholly unsuited to any arid region. The homestead law[12] gave a man 160 acres of land and presumed that he should not acquire more. Since a man could not live on 160 acres of land in many parts of the region, he had to acquire more or starve. Men **circumvented**[13] this law in every possible way, and managed at last to build up estates sufficient to yield a living. Major Powell[14] pointed out that the land unit in the arid region should be 2650 acres, instead of 160 as in the East. But the lawmakers could never see the force of the argument.

The law of water illustrates with peculiar force the unsuitableness of the old law. The English common law and the common law as applied in the East prohibited the diversion of water from a stream or limited it so rigidly that it amounted to a prohibition. The English

---

[11] **maverick**—unbranded range animal.

[12] homestead law—Homestead Act of 1862, which provided 160-acre parcels of public land in the West free to settlers willing to farm them.

[13] **circumvented**—got around.

[14] Major Powell—John Wesley Powell (1834–1902), U.S. geologist and ethnologist who explored the Southwest.

common law, strictly enforced, **precluded**[15] all possibility of irrigation on an extensive scale. The Westerner violated the law, and finally evolved a new one known as the arid-region doctrine of prior appropriation. . . .

In the proposed fence legislation, before the invention or extensive use of barbed wire, we see another example of what might be called anti-Plains legislation. In the East men had been in the habit of fencing their crops. When the agricultural frontier emerged on the Plains and it was found to be impossible to build fences, the farmers immediately tried to cure their trouble by legislation. They agitated for a law which would compel men (in this case the cattlemen) to fence their stock so that the farmer could let the fields lie out. The law was actually passed in Texas, though it was made a matter of local option.[16] Eastern Texas counties required that stock be fenced; the western Texas counties, of course, kept the open range. A similar law was passed in regard to carrying a six-shooter. Eastern Texas prohibited it; western Texas was permitted to carry the six-shooter as long as the Indians were there. Any law forbidding it would have been violated. . . .

Therefore the West was a lawless place. It was turbulent in the early days because there was no law. It was lawless in the later period because the laws were unsuited to the needs and conditions. Men could not abide by them and survive. Not only were absurd laws imposed upon them, but their customs, which might well have received the sanction of law, were too seldom recognized. The blame for a great deal of Western lawlessness rests more with the lawmaker than with the lawbreaker.

If the character of the West was . . . lawless, its reputation for being so outran the facts. No other part of the frontier enjoyed the publicity that was given to the West. There are several reasons for this. First, the West was late

---

[15] **precluded**—prevented.

[16] a matter of local option—communities could decide for themselves how or whether to follow the law.

in developing, and its development came at a time of peace. The nation had become strong enough to handle its own internal affairs with conscious strength, but it had not yet begun its vigorous foreign policy of imperial expansion. Its whole attention was centered on itself. The West was the last stronghold of the frontier to be reduced, and therefore it loomed high on the egocentric national horizon. The nation could throw its whole strength into the fray.[17] Secondly, the West differed from the other sections in its relation to the path of migration. When the Southern man migrated he moved west but remained in the South; when the Northern man migrated he remained in the North. There was comparatively little movement north and south. There was little common experience until the two invading columns of immigrants struck the Great Plains, where both the Northern men and the Southern men found themselves out of their own section. For the first time they met common problems, whether in western Texas or in North Dakota. There was no North or South in the West. When these men wrote home or returned on a visit, they told a *common* story; for once they agreed. The whole nation came to look on the West in the same way as to Indians, as to cattle, later as to wheat and dry farming, as to its . . . lawlessness. Thirdly, the Great Plains frontier developed after the means of rapid communication and transportation were highly perfected. The railroads pushed through the land when life was still wild—when the trains were blocked by buffalo herds, and the section hands had to fight Indians as well as dig ditches and lay rails and crossties. The newspapers had developed, the telegraph flashed the news of Indian fights and train robberies all over the nation, and the newspapers carried the accounts to the breakfast table of millions. The Great Plains frontier was a national frontier, nationally advertised. What happened there was magnified in the

---

[17] fray—fight; conflict.

press and exaggerated in the imagination, and nothing was more magnified than its . . . lawlessness.

Why is the West politically Radical?

The radicalism[18] of the Great Plains is but a continuation of that "lawlessness" discussed [earlier], and it arises in part from the same causes. It is the result of an effort at adjustment through political action to new conditions, a searching for the solution of problems where the old formulas fail and the new ones are unknown. The political radicalism has arisen partly from discontent born of suffering.

It may be said, parenthetically, that the political radicalism and innovation of the Great Plains belong primarily if not wholly to the later agricultural period. There is no record of its existence among the men of the cattle kingdom. They accepted the country as God made it, and wanted to keep it in the hands of "God, the government, and us." When the government began a series of legislative acts which dispossessed them or attempted to dispossess them, and turned the country over to the farmers, the cattlemen protested personally, but they never resorted to political action. They were so few in number that they probably could not have made themselves heard.

Political radicalism on the Plains began with the farmers. The prairie region of the Great Plains has been the stronghold of the farmers' movement. Regardless of where the movements began, they always gained their greatest membership in the prairie and Plains region. This was true of the Grange, the Farmers' Alliance, the Farmers' Union, the Nonpartisan League. The Populist party was reënforced from the Great Plains, and the most radical innovator of the Democratic party, William Jennings Bryan,[19] was from Nebraska. His "You shall not press

---

[18] radicalism—approach to political issues that favors major change from traditional solutions, usually applied to socialist or communist approaches.

[19] William Jennings Bryan (1860–1925)—congressman who gave this famous speech against the gold standard at the Democratic national convention of 1896.

down upon the brow of labor this crown of thorns" may have been inspired by the suffering and poverty which he saw among the homesteaders on the Nebraska plains.

Radicalism is the political expression of economic **maladjustment**.[20] It has been made clear in the preceding pages that the farmers in the prairies and the Great Plains confronted terrible obstacles. They were far from markets, burned by drought, beaten by hail, withered by hot winds, frozen by blizzards, eaten out by the grasshoppers, exploited by capitalists, and cozened[21] by politicians. Why should they not turn to radicalism? When men suffer, they become politically radical; when they cease to suffer, they favor the existing order. Here is a story that will illustrate:

There was in a certain Western state a community of farmers who were undertaking to farm on alkali land.[22] They became infected by socialistic doctrines, and practically the entire community became socialistic. In the summer the people would hold encampments, bringing speakers from far and near, and neglect their suffering crops to **harangue**[23] at the government and **berate**[24] the capitalists. There was nothing vicious about them. They were small landowners who had been caught in the grip of Plains circumstances. Whether or not the mood would have passed by, or whether some new cult would have routed the old one, it is impossible to say. What happened was that oil was discovered in the region, and the whole country found itself in the throes of an oil boom of the most extravagant nature. Money flowed like water, and practically every landowner in the county received for leases and sales of royalty or in fee more money than he ever dreamed of having. If oil were found on his land, his wealth became to him incalculable. From that day until

---

[20] **maladjustment**—distress; failure.

[21] cozened—deceived.

[22] alkali land—land containing mineral salts and hence not acidic enough to grow crops.

[23] **harangue**—make speeches.

[24] **berate**—scold.

this no word of socialistic doctrine has been heard from any of these people. Wealth or comparative wealth dissolved all those troubles they hoped to cure by radicalism.

Woman's **suffrage**[25] does not now come under the head of political radicalism, but it was so considered until a few years ago. With the American Revolution the **franchise**[26] was granted to the common man, provided he was not too common. After the Civil War it was granted to the Negro, and in 1920 it was granted to women. If we examine the history of the woman's movement, we find that it spread practically all over the Great Plains before it was adopted in the East. The map tells the story; it makes clear what happened, but it does not explain why it happened.

---

[25] **suffrage**—right of voting.

[26] **franchise**—right to vote.

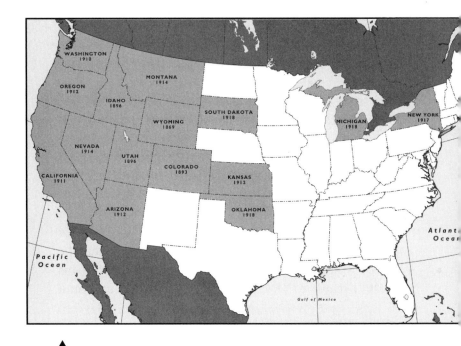

▲

In the shaded states, women could already vote in state elections when the Nineteenth Amendment was passed in 1920. Dates indicate the year in which suffrage was obtained.

Why the men of the West were the first to grant the women the franchise is a problem that remains to be solved. Its final solution will grow out of a better understanding of a peculiar psychology which developed in a region where population was sparse and women were comparatively scarce and remarkably self-reliant. It was not the vaunted[27] chivalry of the South nor the cool justice of the Brahman[28] of the North that gave women the ballot. There is hidden somewhere in the cause the spirit of the Great Plains which made men democratic in deed and in truth.

What has been the Spiritual Effect of the American Adventure in the Great Plains on Women?

Since practically this whole study has been devoted to the men, they will receive scant attention here. The Great Plains in the early period was strictly a man's country—more of a man's country than any other portion of the frontier. Men loved the Plains, or at least those who stayed there did. There was zest to the life, adventure in the air, freedom from restraint; men developed a hardihood which made them insensible to the hardships and lack of refinements. But what of the women? Most of the evidence, such as it is, reveals that the Plains repelled the women as they attracted the men. There was too much of the unknown, too few of the things they loved. If we could get at the truth we should doubtless find that many a family was stopped on the edge of the timber by women who refused to go farther. A student relates that his family migrated from the East to Missouri with a view of going farther into the West, and that when the women caught sight of the Plains they refused to go farther, and the family turned south and settled in the edge of the timbered country, where the children still reside. That family is significant.

---

[27] vaunted—widely praised or boasted about.

[28] Brahman—elite.

Literature is filled with women's fear and distrust of the Plains. It is all expressed in Beret Hansa's[29] pathetic exclamation, "Why, there isn't even a thing that one can *hide behind!*" No privacy, no friendly tree—nothing but earth, sky, grass, and wind. The loneliness which women endured on the Great Plains must have been such as to crush the soul, provided one did not meet the isolation with an adventurous spirit. The woman who said that she could always tell by sunup whether she should have company during the day is an example. If in the early morning she could detect a cloud of dust, she knew that visitors were coming! Exaggeration, no doubt, but suggestive. The early conditions on the Plains precluded the little luxuries that women love and that are so necessary to them. Imagine a sensitive woman set down on an arid plain to live in a dugout or a pole pen with a dirt floor, without furniture, music, or pictures, with the bare necessities of life! No trees or shrubbery or flowers, little water, plenty of sand and high wind. The wind alone drove some to the **verge**[30] of insanity and caused others to migrate in time to avert the tragedy. The few women in the cattle kingdom led a lonely life, but one that was not without its compensations. The women were few; and every man was a self-appointed protector of women who participated in the adventures of the men and escaped much of the drabness and misery of farm life. The life of the farm woman was intolerable, unutterably lonely. If one may judge by fiction, one must conclude that the Plains exerted a peculiarly appalling effect on women. Does this fiction reflect a truth or is it merely the imagining of the authors? One who has lived on the Plains, especially in the pioneer period, must realize that there is much truth in the fiction. The wind, the sand, the

---

[29] Beret Hansa—character in Ole Rölvaag's novel *Giants in the Earth* (1927), which describes the harsh life of Norwegian immigrants farming in South Dakota.

[30] **verge**—edge.

drought, the **unmitigated**[31] sun, and the boundless expanse of a horizon on which danced fantastic images conjured up by the mirages, seemed to overwhelm the women with a sense of desolation, insecurity, and futility, which they did not feel when surrounded with hills and green trees. Who can tell us how the Great Plains affected women, and why?

---

[31] **unmitigated**—unrelieved.

QUESTIONS TO CONSIDER

1. According to Webb, why was the West lawless?

2. Why was the Homestead Act unsuited to arid regions?

3. Webb observed, "There was no North or South in the West." What did he mean?

4. What contributed to the political radicalism of Western farmers?

5. How did the success of the woman's suffrage movement illustrate Western political radicalism?

6. According to Webb, why were women repelled by the Great Plains?

A Saga of Families

BY KATHLEEN NEILS CONZEN

*Some of the most influential intepretations of the history of the
American West have been provided by the movies, and no
Hollywood director is more closely associated with westerns than
John Ford (1895–1973). In an article exploring the role of families
in the development of the West, historian Kathleen Neils Conzen
begins examining the themes of "family, kinship, and community" in*
My Darling Clementine, *Ford's classic film version of the gunfight
at the O.K. Corral (page 97).*

A family story lies at the heart of American western
history. Through the oft-told tales of western conquest
and resistance, settlement and development, wind subtle, insistent themes of family, **kinship**,[1] and community.
Consider, for example, one extraordinarily evocative
scene from *My Darling Clementine,* John Ford's classic
1946 western film starring Henry Fonda as Wyatt Earp.
Silhouetted against the bright southwestern sky rises the
skeletal frame of a church tower, a cross at its peak, a

---

[1] **kinship**—connection by blood, marriage, or adoption.

joyous bell pealing from its topmost rafters. A lowering mesa broods in the background, nature dwarfing the raw town at its base. In the foreground, two American flags whip bravely in the brisk wind. Men, women, and children, all dressed in their Sunday best, crowd onto the plank floor of the unfinished meetinghouse. And in their midst, knees awkwardly lifted in cautious celebration of the new church, dances the town's tough, gunfighting, poker-playing marshal, tamed by the genteel[2] Bostonian whom he holds **gingerly**[3] in his arms.

Ford's haunting imagery encapsulates[4] one of the primal[5] themes in the history and mythology of the nineteenth-century American West. Time and again, in memoirs and novels, folk songs and films, political speeches and academic histories, Americans have insisted that the story of western settlement is a story of the conquest of nature and the taming of human nature in the name of the family and of the community that families together form. In this familiar saga, the **trajectory**[6] from savagery to civilization both defines and legitimates the westward expansion of the American people, and the essence of American civilization lies in its institutions of family and community life. The western drama may seem to be a violent, masculine one, its main protagonists[7] almost exclusively male. Mountain men and miners, cowboys and speculators, native warriors and the U.S. Cavalry, all crowd onto center stage. But sooner or later even the most relentlessly masculine conquest narrative yields to the developmental logic of domestication,[8] and the spotlight shifts to those other archetypal[9] figures who

---

[2] genteel—refined; well-mannered.

[3] **gingerly**—cautiously; carefully.

[4] encapsulates—summarizes.

[5] primal—basic.

[6] **trajectory**—path.

[7] protagonists—characters.

[8] developmental logic of domestication—necessary growth of family life.

[9] archetypal—essential.

have been waiting in the wings—families trekking westward in covered wagons, wives working alongside husbands to erect a log cabin, warriors setting their hands to the plow, children trudging to a one-room schoolhouse, a community building a church. In popular perception and scholarly interpretation alike, the final integration of the western saga into the nation's ongoing history always seems to turn on those pregnant[10] moments when family and community finally take root, just as Ford's turbulent film pivots on the gentle scene at the church dance.

Thus when Ford's boomtown marshal, the fictionalized Wyatt Earp, symbolically embraces the communal and familial values represented by the newly formed Tombstone congregation and by Clementine, the lady from Boston, his feud with the vicious Clantons becomes a crusade for civilization and his success at the O.K. Corral a bittersweet victory that brings to an end the only way of life in which he, with his shooter's skills, could flourish. Ford establishes the essential savagery of both nature and man at the opening of the film with stark camera shots of a pair of menacing gunmen who observe cattle and cowboys in a parched desert setting. But at the end of the film it is a woman, Clementine, the town's new schoolteacher, standing by a tamed, fenced-in landscape, who takes the observer's role as the shooters depart.

The three Earps, seeking to avenge their murdered youngest brother, initially encounter a darkly lit Tombstone of saloons, dance halls, and poker games, a world where Shakespearean tragedians can only degenerate into farce.[11] "Wide-awake, wide-open town, Tombstone! You can get anything you want there." Its **denizens**[12] are rowdy miners and cowboys, gamblers

---

[10] pregnant—meaningful.

[11] degenerate into farce—decline into low comedy.

[12] **denizens**—inhabitants.

and whores, its boss a consumptive,[13] alcoholic physician who has turned his back on the civilization of the East. Clementine, his former fiancee, proves unable to reclaim Doc Holliday for Boston and all it stands for. But she begins the taming of Wyatt Earp, and as he primps for her in the local barbershop, Ford lets us glimpse for the first time a different, brighter Tombstone. Beyond the dark of the hotel porch the street floods with sunshine. Wagons and buggies purposefully stream past, families greet one another on the sidewalk, and serving girls in their best hats bustle out of the hotel. "If I wasn't in the territory," Virgil Earp observes, "I'd swear we were back home on a Sunday morning." But the Sabbath has indeed come to the territory. "You know," says Morgan Earp, "there's probably a lot of nice people around here. We just ain't met 'em." Then Wyatt accepts Clementine's ladylike challenge to escort her to church; he slowly leaves the shadows to step with her out into the Sabbath sun. Thus when the Earps subsequently destroy the Clantons at the O.K. Corral, they not only have avenged their brother; they have also, as Wyatt promised, left behind a country where young kids like him "will be able to grow up and live safe," where law and culture are free from ridicule, where the schoolteacher literally replaces the gunslinger. Female sexuality yields to feminine sensibility,[14] and the madam shows herself to be a sensitive nurse. Even Doc Holliday, although too corrupted to be allowed to survive into the new era, is redeemed in death by his belated decision to join Wyatt's crusade.

At the heart of the western saga, Ford would appear to be telling us, lies the civilizing process. The Wild West is an individualistic, solipsistic[15] male world untrammeled[16] by law, morality, higher culture, or feminine domesticity.

---

[13] consumptive—suffering from tuberculosis.

[14] feminine sensibility—womanly feelings.

[15] solipsistic—self-willed.

[16] untrammeled—unrestricted.

Its women are deceiving whores and half-breeds, fully deserving the symbolic cleansing in the horse trough that Wyatt administers to Chihuahua, Doc's paramour.[17] Domesticity is as doomed as young James Earp and his plans to marry his sweetheart. "Mac, you ever been in love?" Wyatt asks one of Doc's employees. "No," he replies, "I been a bartender all me life." Women, the family, and the bonds of community can thrive, it seems, only when the West has been tamed. They are the motive that invests the history of western violence with virtue, just as their ultimate triumph signals the end of the uniquely western experience and the final integration of the frontier into the ongoing history of the settled, civilized nation. And in the process they are themselves changed, strengthened, made more **robust**.[18] A formerly dependent woman like Clementine can now stand alone and shape a role for herself in constructing the new community; the community, like the deacon's womenfolk, can reject the artificial conventions of the East for the wholesome naturalness of western life. Family and community, fresh and reinvigorated, are the rewards that lie at the end of the trail, the ends but not the means[19] of western conquest.

Or are they? Ford's story on one level is indeed the familiar **parable**[20] of family, community, and the civilizing process that has provided so much of western legend and history with its standard plot. But on another level it charts what can be understood only as a far more complex transformation from one **regime**[21] of family and community to another. The Clantons, after all, are in Ford's telling also a family of a kind, a dynasty of four brothers held together by their father's will and whip,

---

[17] paramour—lover.

[18] **robust**—healthy.

[19] ends...means—goals but not methods.

[20] **parable**—story with a moral lesson; fable.

[21] **regime**—rule; government.

and the Earps are yet another set of apparently mother-less sons, bound in duty and affection to the family economy headed by their Pa back in California. Powerful motives of family honor and vengeance fuel the actions of both clans. Not even Doc Holliday has fully shaken off the claims of family and community. Rather, he is a **renegade**[22] who prolongs his exile to avoid bringing shame to those who claim him as their own, and in his resistance to the new regime that Clementine represents he even contemplates making his liaison[23] with Chihuahua a permanent one.

Nor is Ford's **raucous**[24] Tombstone without its own communal structures.[25] It has a mayor and a marshal and the forms of law; when Wyatt Earp marches to the O.K. Corral, he does so with an arrest warrant in his pocket and with the blessings of both the mayor and the deacon of the new church. Untamed Tombstone can con-stitute itself a moral community in quest of common goals, whether simple entertainment or support for a wounded singer. And it is linked to the wider national community by everything from accounts in the Lordsburg bank to newfangled barber chairs imported from Kansas City. It may not share the moral code of the domesticated, cultured East, but it has its own commu-nal morality nonetheless, a masculine morality that **proscribes**[26] equally stealing cattle, playing eight-handed poker games, cheating on one's lover, and drawing on a man who is not carrying a gun. Ford's **ambivalence**[27] about the passing of this order may not be as **palpable**[28] here as in a later film like *The Man Who*

---

[22] **renegade**—outlaw; rebel.

[23] liaison—relationship.

[24] **raucous**—disorderly.

[25] communal structures—community institutions; local government.

[26] **proscribes**—outlaws.

[27] **ambivalence**—contradictory feelings.

[28] **palpable**—obvious; easy to perceive.

Shot Liberty Valance (1962), with its **overt**[29] acknowledgment of the falsity of the myths upon which the civilizing process rested. But when Wyatt Earp rides away from Tombstone and its new teacher, it is not just Clementine who is "lost and gone forever" to him. In remaining true to the **dictates**[30] of one kind of family and community, he has midwifed[31] another, different familial, communal order in which a man like himself can find no place. It is not so much that family and community triumph as that one kind of family order replaces another.

Ford's story, of course, bears only a **tenuous**[32] relationship to historical reality. It is rather difficult to turn the actual saga of the Earps, the Clantons, Doc Holliday, and the O.K. Corral into a comparable drama of domestication, no matter how **ambiguous**.[33] The historical Earps were hardly the virtuous retired lawmen and cowboys of Ford's fable. The best recent accounts make it clear that the Earps, though probably not the stage robbers and horse thieves of the revisionist counterlegend,[34] were definitely gamblers, bartenders, brothel keepers, and small-time speculators, as well as sometime lawmen and farmers. The famous shoot-out—not at, but near, the O.K. Corral—had less to do with family vengeance than with tensions arising from economic and political rivalry. And rather than nobly sacrificing his life, Doc Holliday—a Georgian, not a Bostonian—probably initiated the slaughter by drawing first, and lived to trade on his **notoriety**.[35] Tombstone indeed had a young, single schoolteacher, twenty-four-year-old Lucy McFarland

---

[29] **overt**—open and observable.

[30] **dictates**—rules.

[31] midwifed—helped give birth to.

[32] **tenuous**—flimsy.

[33] **ambiguous**—open to several interpretations.

[34] revisionist counterlegend—Conzen means an antiheroic picture of the Earps put forward by revisionist historians.

[35] **notoriety**—ill fame.

who lived with her sister and her lawyer brother-in-law, but she was from West Virginia, not Boston, and it was not she but the undoubtedly less virtuous Josephine Sarah Marcus, an "artiste" raised in a prosperous German Jewish mercantile family of San Francisco, who attracted Wyatt Earp's wandering eye.

Nevertheless, like their filmic counterfeits, the real Earps inhabited a West defined by distinctive bonds of family and community. They were the offspring of an agrarian Kentucky clan who migrated westward as a family in chainwise fashion, first to Illinois and Iowa, then to Missouri, Kansas, and California, as the various brothers peeled off on a series of continually intersecting trajectories that carried them singly or together through mining camps, railheads, and cow towns from Montana to Kansas and Texas before reuniting them all in 1880 in the new Arizona boomtown of Tombstone. They were, in fact, all married men. Each arrived in Tombstone with his wife, common-law[36] or otherwise, firmly in tow, though Wyatt would replace his partner with Josie during his Tombstone stay. Their women labored for them and moved with them. The Earp brothers were on occasion founding members of church congregations and candidates for public office. They supported and leaned on one another in their efforts for economic advancement, and outside the O.K. Corral they joined to affirm their reputations against not one but two pairs of brothers—McLaurys as well as Clantons—who like them were striving to make it family-fashion in the West. The Clantons, like the Earps, were members of a southern clan seeking to reproduce a familiar pastoral lifestyle in the new territory. The McLaurys, by contrast, were young New York-born, Iowa-raised **entrepreneurs**[37] who cut loose from their parents to find the fortune that

---

[36] common-law—married by mutual agreement, rather than in a formal civil or religious ceremony.

[37] **entrepreneurs**—those engaged in independent business ventures.

would enable them to found new families of their own. Doc Holliday's initial move west can be seen as a similar attempt by the professional son of well-to-do urban, middle-class parents to establish a home for himself in a healthier climate. The real Tombstone, like its movie version, was overwhelmingly a community of unattached miners leavened[38] by a sprinkling of families like these, to be found mainly within the town's small entrepreneurial class. But the surrounding countryside was punctuated with smaller, family-centered communities—one of them Mormon, several Mexican—that testified to the area's older, deeper domestic roots. And although the only Native American in Ford's film was the drunkard whose literal removal signaled the beginning of Wyatt Earp's crusade to civilize Tombstone, the constant threat of Apache attack was a disturbing reminder to the historical Tombstone of yet another familial tradition in the region.

---

[38] leavened—modified.

QUESTIONS TO CONSIDER

1. What is the theme of Ford's *My Darling Clementine?*

2. Why is the scene in which Wyatt Earp dances with Clementine "pivotal" to the development of this theme?

3. What value system exists in Tombstone at the outset of the film?

4. In what different ways have the Earps been presented by historians?

The Wild West

▲
Across The Continent, a Currier & Ives print from 1868, presents an idealized vision of settlement following the railroads across the West.

▲
One of the pre-eminent artistic interpreters of the American West, Frederic Remington (1861–1909) created an influential gallery of western types, as in his drawing *Arizona Cowboy* (1901).

▲
"Cowboy artist" Charles M. Russell (1864–1926) drew on his youthful experiences as a wrangler in creating images such as his painting *Buccaroos* (1905).

▲
A darker view of frontier life is presented in Remington's drawing *A Quarrel over Cards—A Sketch from a New Mexico Ranch.*

A poster advertising an 1896 melodrama, *The Great Train Robbery,* shows a greenhorn (a newcomer unaware of local customs) taming a western tough. ▶

Chronology

A.D. 1000—Hopi establish settlements in the Southwest.

1528–1537—Cabeza de Vaca and three companions explore the Southwest.

1539–1542—Coronado Expedition explores the Great Plains, reintroducing horses to the Americas.

1598—Oñate begins Spanish colonization of New Mexico.

1610—Spanish found Santa Fe as capital of New Mexico.

1680—Popé leads Pueblo Indians in revolt, expelling Spanish from New Mexico; Spanish rule not fully restored until 1696.

1769—First Spanish mission founded in California.

1803—France sells the Louisiana Territory to United States.

1804–1806—Lewis and Clark Expedition explores Louisana Territory.

1821—Stephen Austin and U.S. settlers arrive in Texas.

1830s—Artists George Catlin and Karl Bodmer record American Indian life on the Great Plains.

1836—Texans revolt against Mexico, fight battles at Alamo and San Jacinto, establish Lone Star Republic.

1838—Cherokee make forced migration, known as Trail of Tears, to what is now Oklahoma.

1842—First emigrant train travels over Oregon Trail.

1843—United States annexes Texas.

1846–1848—War fought between the United States and Mexico.

1847—Mormons establish Salt Lake City.

1848—Treaty with British establishes Oregon border at 49th parallel; Donner Party trapped by winter in the Sierra Nevadas; Treaty of Guadelupe Hidalgo acknowledges U.S. title to Texas, New Mexico, and California; gold discovered in California, prompting massive gold rush.

1850—Under Compromise of 1850, California enters Union as free state.

1853—Gadsden Purchase establishes present U.S. southwestern border.

1862—Homestead Act passed.

1867—First Texas longhorns driven up the Chisholm Trail to Abilene, Kansas.

1869—Transcontinental railroad completed at Promontory, Utah.

1871—Artist Thomas Moran paints in Yellowstone country.

1872—Yellowstone National Park created.

1876—Lakota defeat Custer at the Battle of the Little Bighorn.

1881—Gunfight takes place behind the O.K. Corral in Tombstone, Arizona; *A Century of Dishonor*, Helen Hunt Jackson's account of mistreatment of Indians, published.

1882—Chinese Exclusion Act passed.

1886—Fewer than 600 buffalo survive.

1889—Western artist Frederic Remington begins career.

1890—Massacre of Lakota Ghost Dancers at Wounded Knee ends resistance of Plains Indians.

1892—John Muir founds Sierra Club; Populist Party convention proposes reforms to aid farmers.

1893—Frederick Jackson Turner presents landmark theory in "The Significance of the Frontier in American History"; "cowboy artist" Charles M. Russell begins full-time career.

1901—Oil discovered at Spindletop in Texas.

1902—National Reclamation Act passed to fund dams and irrigation.

1903—*The Great Train Robbery*, the first western, filmed—in New Jersey.

1904—*The Great Plains* by Walter Prescott Webb published.

1946—*My Darling Clementine*, John Ford's classic film about the gunfight at the O.K. Corral, released.

1987—*The Legacy of Conquest*, Patricia Nelson Limerick's revisionist history of the West, published.

ACKNOWLEDGEMENTS

Texts

16 "The Four Migrations", from *Book Of The Hopi* by Frank Waters, copyright © 1963 by Frank Waters. Used by permission of Viking Penguin, a division of Penguin Putnam Inc.

86 From "A Woman's Trip Across the Plains in 1849" Manuscript Diary by Catherine Haun, from *Women's Diaries of the Westward Journey* by Lillian Schlissel. This item is reproduced by permission of The Huntington Library, San Marino, California.

172 Reprinted from *Land of the Spotted Eagle* by Luther Standing Bear by permission of the University of Nebraska Press. Copyright, 1933, by Luther Standing Bear. Renewal copyright, 1960 by May Jones.

192 From *The Great Plains* by Walter Prescott Webb. Copyright 1931, 1959 by Walter Prescott Webb. Reprinted by permission of Addison-Wesley Educational Publishers, Inc.

206 "A Saga of Families" by Kathleen Neils Conzen, from *The Oxford History Of The American West,* edited by Clyde A. Milner, II, et al, copyright © 1994 by Oxford University Press, Inc. Used by permission of Oxford University Press, Inc.

Images:

Photo Research Diane Hamilton

51–52, 54–56, 109–112, 113 *bottom,* **114, 146–152, 180–186, 215–219** Courtesy of the Library of Congress.

53 National Museum of America Art, Washington DC / Art Resource, NY.

107–108, 113 *top* Courtesy of the National Archives.

Every effort has been made to secure complete rights and permissions for each selection presented herein. Updated acknowledgements, if needed, will appear in subsequent printings.

Index

"African Americans in Oklahoma Territory" 102

Beckwourth, James P. 40

Bird, Isabella 47

Bradbury, John 35

Breen, Patrick 72

Catlin, George 154

"Cattle Drives" 122

Century of Dishonor, A 160

"Chinese Exclusion Act" 130

"Chinese Workers" 127

Clappe, Louisa 116

"Colter's Run" 35

"Conservation of Natural Resources, The" 167

Conzen, Kathleen Neils 206

de Castañeda, Pedro 20

"Destruction of the Buffalo" 133

Dodge, Grenville M. 127

"Donner Party, The" 72

"Early Texas" 66

English-Chinese Phrase Book, An 128

"Expedition of Lewis and Clark, The" 25

"Farming on the Great Plains" 138

Garland, Hamlin 138

Great Plains, The 194

"Gunfight at the O.K. Corral" 97

Haun, Catherine 83

How We Built the Union Pacific Railroad 127

"Indian View of Nature, The" 172

Jackson, Helen Hunt 160

Jefferson, Thomas 25, 31

Journey of Coronado, The 20

"Letters and Notes on the North American Indians" 154

Lewis, Meriwether 25, 31

"Living with the Indians" 40

Mayer, Frank H. 133

McCoy, Joseph G. 122

Migrations of the Hopi, The 16

"Mining in California" 116

"Mormon Migration, The" 76

"Mountain Jim" 47

Mountains of California, The 12

Muir, John 12

Roosevelt, Theodore 167, 184

"Saga of Families, A" 206

"Significance of the Frontier in American History, The" 188

"Spanish California" 58

Standing Bear, Luther 172

Turner, Frederick Jackson 188

Vallejo, Guadalupe 58

Van Zandt, Francis Cook Lipscomb 66

Washington, Booker T. 102

Waters, Frank 16

Webb, Walter Prescott 194

"Woman's Trip Across the Plains in 1849, A" 83

Young, Brigham 76